Jean Adhémar

TWENTIETH-CENTURY GRAPHICS

Translated from the French by
Eveline Hart

PRAEGER PUBLISHERS

New York · Washington

The translator and publisher wish to thank the artist Clifford Hall
for his valuable advice on a number of aspects of the book , and
particularly on the rendering of technical terms into English.

BOOKS THAT MATTER

Published in the United States of America in 1971
by Praeger Publishers, Inc.

111 Fourth Avenue, New York, N.Y. 10003

This translation © 1971 in London, England, by Elek Books Limited

© Original French edition in Paris, France, by Editions Aimery Somogy
Reproduction rights by Spadem and A.D.A.G.P.

Library of Congress Catalog Card Number : 72-150453

Printed in France

TWENTIETH-CENTURY GRAPHICS

CONTENTS

PREFACE

'A work which is to become a classic
will not look like the classics which
preceded it.' PICASSO

Writing a book on twentieth-century graphic art is not an easy task.
For, except in an ever smaller number of cases, prints are the works of painters
and, being done for the artist's own pleasure, often without any intention of
selling them, they remain unknown. This was already the case in the nineteenth
century: a copper etching by Corot was found in an old nail-box long after
the master's death. And in the twentieth century, Picasso's *Frugal Meal*, for
example, executed in 1905, only became known to the public and to other
artists in 1945. Thus, in spite of everything, our information remains
fragmentary, and an unknown masterpiece may change our outlook on prints
when it is discovered twenty years hence. Another factor also makes it
difficult to draw conclusions: the paucity of works on prints: a few books,
occasional reports of exhibitions and haphazard articles and interviews in the
press. Moreover, few exhibitions have shown prints outside their country
of origin, and those few, being official exhibitions, seem to have laid stress
on the more conformist aspects rather than seeking originality.

Yet prints have an immense range, and represent for all of us a vast number
of images, touching on all aspects of our lives. Prints include line engravings
and etchings, but also mezzotint which is coming back into favour, silk-screen
printing whose importance has been recently underlined by a Congress of

7

silk-screen printers, lithography as done by the masters and their printers, book illustrations and, finally, a form of sculpture, the plaster print.

The present school of print making is flourishing, particularly in France, and it would be out of the question to give a list of honours, to cite the very great number of artist engravers we know and respect, and whose talent we admire. Very reluctantly we have had to limit ourselves to the analysis of general movements and to the study in some detail of a few great masters; the extent of this book did not allow for more. Our intention is to show the chronological development of the art, and to consider each artist at the time or times when he was at his most original, when he published the print which represents his most remarkable message. Thus, an artist who produced a masterpiece late in life will not be mentioned with his generation; another who, like Picasso, changed his style several times, will reappear in several different parts of the book.

Our predecessors have frequently erred in evaluating artists, and one is often horrified when reading their books; tastes change, and vary from person to person. Ours will be questioned, but the reader must admit that we have tried to be objective most of the time, to be historians recording facts without, generally speaking, wanting to take sides. But there are things we like and defend, for it is not permissible to speak of art as of mere documents. Lastly, the reader should not mind our starting the history of the twentieth century with the 1890 generation. The twentieth century did not begin in 1900, neither did the eighteenth century begin in 1700, nor the nineteenth in 1800, but a decade or so earlier. Thus we were obliged to go a little further back in time.

Part One

THE BEGINNINGS OF MODERN PRINT MAKING

THE METHODS: LINE ENGRAVING, ETCHING, LITHOGRAPHY, WOOD ENGRAVING

The twentieth century begins around 1890 rather than in 1900, and if we are to understand the complicated sequence of its different movements we must look back to the influences that formed the generation of 1890—which in France takes us to the last few years of the Second Empire (it is true to say that the renaissance in print making of the 1890s started as an almost exclusively French affair, though it spread very quickly to Germany). If we take a close look at the state of the various techniques at this time—line engraving, etching, lithography, wood engraving—we shall see what a revelation and what a decisive influence the art of Whistler was.

At the period in question, the public had turned its back on engraving, as Baudelaire, who was always closely in touch, noted. 'Into what disrepute the noble art of engraving has fallen!' he wrote. 'Where are the days when, after a new plate was announced, collectors used to come and put their names down in advance for the first proofs?' A Parisian columnist of the day bears out Baudelaire's assertion; this is how he reports the conversation of people visiting the Salon: '"Let's not go that way, it's to the engravings. Do you know, there's someone looking at the engravings! No, really!" And they troop upstairs to witness this unusual phenomenon.' Exhibitions of engravings served chiefly as a convenient refuge for lovers in search of solitude.

The reason for this eclipse of engraving is to be found in the sudden, all-conquering vogue of photography.

Photography, which as early as 1855 was exhibited as an art form at the Salon, brought about a complete revolution, for it could be used to reproduce not only faces but pictures. Engravers were very apprehensive of this latter function, since the accuracy of photographic reproduction was being extolled at the expense of engraving, which is only able, and only intended, to give a somewhat free interpretation of the original. Engravers were bewildered. One of the foremost among them, Félix Bracquemond gives a good idea of their dismay: 'Photography has brought disruption to all that pertains to the art and craft of engraving. Disruption is hardly the word, considering this new wonder is doing away with engraving altogether.' There was much indignation. Monsieur de Saint Arroman rose up in arms against the partisans of photography: The *cliché* is about to replace everything in art as well as in literature. Every day I come across people who look as if they were in their right minds, people like you and me, and these people candidly prefer a photograph to an engraving.'

Engravers were indignant and distressed at the loss of their livelihood. They fought but the battle was already lost, although the last of the reproductive engravers were far from dead; the more intelligent among them realized that engraving must take a new path: that of print making, which had already been marked out by the lithographs of Géricault, Delacroix and Corot. Engraving must henceforward be exclusively original engraving. Some engravers began to rejoice as early as 1873: 'Today, now that . . . nature can be projected on paper by anybody capable of operating a camera, artists need no longer be enslaved by all that patient fidelity to detail, all that painstaking imitation. Fancy, ingenuity, fresh personal impressions, these are what are required now—and this is no bad thing.'

During this period the prints which appealed to the widest public and which were most commonly seen were reproductions. These were frequently line engravings, but not always. Photomechanical techniques were used, and different techniques mixed together, and the result was a type of engraving which delighted our forebears (it was called the 'Varin process', after the engraver who used it most in the 1860s, and also 'process engraving').

These engravings were nearly all issued by the same publisher, Goupil, who was enormously successful with a very extensive public. Having good sales, Goupil paid his engravers more than adequately and was able to employ the best craftsmen. His most regular engraver was Henriquel-Dupont, and his appointed painter Paul Delaroche, 'the painter of the middle classes'. Delaroche, as his contemporaries used to say, 'excelled at setting down an idea on canvas'. He gave the public, which craved for them, numerous touching scenes painted expressly to be engraved. Béraldi, describing a bourgeois interior of the 1870s, noted engravings by Henriquel-Dupont after Delaroche in every room of the flat. Henriquel-Dupont was to dominate engraving: in 1863 he was appointed professor of engraving at the Ecole des Beaux-Arts; for forty years under his direction it produced many line engravers in the old tradition, who engraved as in the seventeenth century and upheld the increasingly archaic traditions of their master until as late as 1914.

But not all line engravers followed Henriquel-Dupont. Many rebelled against elaborately worked plates filled with cross-hatching to give an effect of light and shade. They wanted to go back to Dürer with his simple line and his marvellously effective use of the white of the paper in his handling of space. By 1870 they had started a revolution by reverting to simple line engraving. One of the first indications of this change was a man's head after Dürer, engraved by the young Adolf Huot around 1860. Huot wrote at the bottom that he was engraving this work in the manner of Dürer 'so as to seek inspiration from it in [his] future work.' In 1862 Francois Flameng sent an engraving after Ingres' *La Source* to the Salon; in this piece the white paper plays a very large part and journalists said jokingly, 'What I admire most is the part the engraver has left blank.' They sensed that something had changed but hesitated to give the innovator their support. It was still worse the following year, when Claude Gaillard sent to the Salon his *Portrait of Giovanni Bellini*. This young artist, a member of the French school in Rome and winner of the first prize for engraving, was seen by his masters as a deserter and a traitor, and his entry was refused by the jury of the Salon. This revolutionary entry seems still very innocuous to us, yet it cannot be denied that it was the origin of a revolution in line engraving. This revolution was not to be led by Gaillard, however, for he was soon diverted into a blind alley, minutely scrutinizing the human face and trying to reproduce it on plates which

11

competed unsuccessfully with photography until his death in 1887.

After line engravings, etching. Charles Meryon, who revived etching around 1854, died insane in 1868, leaving behind him works which, though few in number, were to have strong repercussions. After him Millet, Rousseau, Daubigny and all the masters of the Barbizon school were to produce etchings and leave us many beautiful etched landscapes.

These artists were fortunate enough to come upon a printer and a publisher. The printer was Auguste Delâtre, who was working as early as 1848; he gave himself to the cause of etching, and the artists, delighted with his skill, swore by him. Seymour Haden even proclaimed that if Rembrandt were to come back to life he would give him his plates to print. Delâtre soon gained a world-wide reputation. People came from everywhere to consult him; and though they may have reproached him for his over-use of effect, they always praised his competence and helpfulness.

The publisher was Cadart, a capable and shrewd businessman, who started by publishing photographs of naked women and later took an interest in etching, publishing almost 600 modern plates in ten years. In 1861 the *Société des Aquafortistes* was established at his house and brought out an annual folio of etchings. Daubigny, Legros, Bonvin, Manet and Jongkind worked for him and secured the reputation of his business. Similar ventures were being embarked on in England: Seymour Haden, Whistler's brother-in-law, tried his hand at etching at the age of forty and was immediately enthusiastic, repeatedly praising the new method and defending it against Ruskin; he asked Delâtre over twice to teach the English its use. But he found himself up against strong opposition, which lasted practically until the end of the nineteenth century. Similarly, in France, etching triumphed over line engraving, but there was long-lasting opposition from line engravers, publishers and the public. Line engravers derided etching for its ease and its sketch-like appearance, and made fun of those 'scrawls' which, according to them, anybody could have done. The publishers and the public also refused to accept these sketches, which they considered lacking in precision and never having the appearance of a *finished* work. The public liked fine, lustrous, highly polished engravings which looked nice on the wall.

Now line engraving, that was something, the public would say: you could make out the subject down to its smallest details. They praised, for example, the works of Meissonier, in which everything was visible, and considered as his masterpiece a certain miniature portrait where the model wore a tie-pin the size of a pin's head, on which an eruption of Vesuvius could be discerned; or another line engraving where the model wore a ring on which a woman appeared who seemed to be pregnant.

But etchers had one force on their side: that of the press. They had the backing of the newspapers and the men of letters; Baudelaire and Théophile Gautier sided with this new mode of expression and after ten years they finally won the contest. In 1873 Burger recorded their triumph: 'Well, the battle is over. Etching, which was virtually abandoned in the eighteenth century, is once more entering the repertoire of French art. It now has a place . . . in the exhibitions and is already arousing the curious and the print collectors. We now have quite a school of etchers.'

Etching was everywhere. Braquemond was practising it and praised it with unequalled enthusiasm; Gaucherel, artistic director of the review *L'Art*, published nothing but etchings in his review; as a member of the Salon jury he strongly defended etchers and had their entries accepted. Félix Buhot, another advocate of etching, made a large number of racy compositions which he printed on different coloured papers, as did Henri Guérard.

Yet etching had one dangerous drawback: its very ease and abundance were prejudicial to it, for everybody wanted to etch and found it possible to do so. Monarchs and princes went in for it: the King of Sweden, the King of Portugal, Princess Mathilda. As Béraldi said, 'Etching is like playing the piano: anyone can play, from Beethoven composing sonatas, down to the child strumming *Au clair de la lune* with one finger.' The unskilful engravers who made up the majority were doing an injustice to the virtuosi who remained the exception. Cadart's publications were for the most part mediocre. The printer played an ever more important part, hiding the imperfections of his clients' works under floods of ink, under a thick *sauce*. Etchings grew darker and darker. Cadart died in 1875 and his widow went bankrupt in 1882.

Another cause of its weakness was that etching was practised by overslick technicians, *cooks* as they were called. Count Lepic, for example, who had the good fortune to sit for Degas, had a method which even his printer found astonishing. He etched a landscape of the banks of the Escault and by using different inking he printed it in eighty-five different ways; it gave a sunset effect, a night effect, a moonrise effect, etc. Yet he boasted that he just used ink and a rag: 'My rag is free to all artists without their having to ask me, and even to all the publishers, who will ask.'

What was most lacking in etching was its use by great artists, by painters of real talent; there was the threat of its being used by reproductive engravers, and it was these who founded the *Société des Aquafortistes français* in 1885. In 1889, however, the painters retorted by founding the *Peintres-Graveurs français,* just preceded in London by the Society of Painter Etchers and Engravers. And so it was the 1890 generation that was to give birth to modern etching.

Meanwhile the art of wood engraving, as is well known, had been renewed by Gustave Doré. Doré would do a wash drawing on a prepared wood block, which the engraver had to reproduce in all its subtlety. This new style, the *Style Doré* as Gustave Doré himself called it, had been very much in vogue: wood engraved in this way was called a tone block. In this method Daniel Vierge, Frédéric Florian, Timothy Cole and Auguste Lepère vied with each other in both talent and output. Tone blocks were used to illustrate books and, most frequently, for news pictures in the papers, notably in the *Monde Illustré.* But around 1880 the tone block became greatly over-refined, seeking with astonishing technical skill 'the height of subtlety, light greys and delicate variations of tone', to quote Gusman, one of its most technically skilled exponents, but only achieving a dull grey image easily outdone by photography. It seemed obvious that wood engraving had reached a dead end.

Rather than spend any longer on line engraving and the wood block, which could have been seen at this point as things of the past, let us examine what chances there were of new departures. First of all, was there a public? Was the public interested in prints? The opinions of contemporaries differed widely on this point. For there were now two sorts of print: artists' prints and engravers' prints.

Engravers' prints sold well; Béraldi wrote: 'Never before has engraving had such an enthusiastic public, so willing to part with its money. Publishers sell artists' proofs by the hundred, proofs of different states, trial proofs, and they all find buyers.' True, but the proliferation of prints in different states diminished the number of collectors, since 'knowing states has become a veritable science. In the past people were not so particular about it; what they cared for most of all was having the block at the height of its beauty . . ., nowadays the first state is the least desirable . . . the last the most important', and collectors hoped that this fine state would soon become rare: 'This consideration of rarity took on such importance in the eyes of collectors that they would often place scarcity value above intrinsic quality.' In 1897 Bracquemond, an oracle with a large audience, gave his approval to connoisseurs in quest of states.

PAINTERS' ENGRAVINGS

Painters' engravings, however, did not have the same wide public. In 1890 Camille Pissarro wrote to his son how he had 'had a long conversation with Dumont, who has a splendid shop in the Rue Laffitte. He never sees a soul. He is most upset. And they say that from New York to London and from London to Paris, there is general indifference to everything to do with the art of engraving. Reproductions alone are appreciated. Goupil's firm sells its *rubbish* in New York and London. Those few exceptions who consider themselves pure art lovers have complete sets of Charles Jacques and Félix Buhot, and among these one or two Seymour Hadens, Whistlers and Legros. But that is all. It is all very sad and not at all encouraging.' In order to come to the rescue of this art form, in 1891 the *Peintres-Graveurs français,* founded in 1889, turned itself into a Society (as French painters and engravers they did not include the 'Ecole de Paris' of that period, but invited Pissarro and Mary Cassatt to join as foreign members. They refused, considering themselves members by right). In 1893 Marty founded the magazine *L'Estampe Originale,* which in spite of its great interest was not very successful; the bookbinder René Wiener devised a magnificent leather portfolio in poker work and mosaic for those who wished to bind their copies, but he could not sell it and he bequeathed it to the Museum of the Ecole de Nancy.

On the other hand, one notices if one studies the etched works of artists, that about 1880 many new ideas were in the air: in particular a return to pure line and the attraction exerted by etching as a medium. All that was wanting was a great, modern and active artist who would produce true works of art and whose example would bring about a modern school and shake off the ancient traditions. This great artist was to be Whistler, whose etched views of Venice in 1880 and lithographs in 1893 imposed a new aesthetic.

WHISTLER

Whistler, after various experiments in painting and etching, left for Italy in 1879, commissioned by the Fine Art Society of London to do twelve etchings of Venice. He stayed fourteen months in Venice and brought back forty etchings, which he exhibited in 1880. They were revolutionary in their choice of subject, since Whistler was not representing the monuments but the dilapidated palazzos, old doorways, gardens, beggars, the water and the sun (subjects taken up by the aesthetes and to be found also in *The Aspern Papers* by Henry James and in the novels of Henri de Regnier which could all have been called, as one of them was, *L'Initiation Vénitienne*). They were still more revolutionary in technique, for the artist did not draw his outlines in unbroken lines but suggested them by short hatchings which also filled in the shadows. For the first time since the fifteenth century, tradition had been abandoned and a new era was dawning. On his return his etchings were printed in London. Sometimes he entrusted them to the printer Goulding, and sometimes he printed them himself. There is a world of difference between the prints pulled by the artist and the rest. Indeed, since a plate by Whistler carried only a few indications and the inking needed very special attention, the pulls made by the artist were infinitely superior to any others; it was very difficult for him to indicate all the finer points to a workman with little conception of the subtleties involved.

At first, the etchings of Venice had no success: accused of being nothing but sketches, working drawings, unfinished works which should have been taken further, they were denied all merit. In England and America the artist was attacked in the press. Seymour Haden tried, by giving lectures in America, to incline the connoisseurs towards his friend, and in 1883 he succeeded. But the general public was still reticent. After his exhibition in

JAMES MACNEILL WHISTLER. *Venice.* 1883. Etching

JAMES MACNEILL WHISTLER. *The Two Doorways.* 1879. Etching

1880 Whistler was considered an *eccentric*. He had exhibited fifty etchings in a gallery painted in yellow and white, where he distributed yellow butterflies to the visitors. He wore yellow socks and made his friends wear ties of the same colour.

Somewhat later, about 1892, Whistler went to Paris. Jacques-Emile Blanche saw him at Degas' house. 'I met him at Degas' . . . He had brought with him a portfolio of drypoints of Venice, which he drew out with infinite precaution from a vellum case with white ribbons. I could not understand at all those wan prints, intricate as reflections in water.' Whistler afterwards became enthusiastic about colour lithography. It is quite likely that he had seen

Lautrec's. In any case he drew numerous lithographs, original in both their inspiration and their technique. He worked out the designs on transfer paper and gave them to his printer to transfer to the stone and pull the prints. (Whistler drew very few of his many lithographs directly on the stone. His printer, Thomas Way, not only transferred and printed most of Whistler's lithographs, but also made colour lithographs after his paintings.) Among Whistler's lithographs we might mention a portrait of Mallarmé which required numerous sittings, after which, as Henri Mondor describes in his book on Mallarmé, 'one day Whistler got in a few lines an intense and fluent likeness of his friend, an impression at once ethereal and profound'. Not only did he preach by example; he was also a theoretician who had interesting and sometimes profound views on the art of engraving. He disallowed the use of mechanical processes, considering the methods of Goupil's engravers as heresy: only acid, the burin and lithography were legitimate. A print should be in black and white; engraving in colours was 'abominable, vulgar and stupid', with the exception of lithography. Apart from this, a print should rely on its own worth; the margin ought not to be ornamented as in the engravings of Buhot. The margin ought not even to exist, for collectors find 'a strange pleasure in the quantity of paper', and Whistler trimmed it right down in his own work, to the great indignation of his publisher. Many of these principles are still valid today.

Walter Richard Sickert, 1860–1942, who had been a pupil both of Whistler and of Degas, produced a great number of etchings. Contrary to Whistler's practice in his later etchings, Sickert's declared aim was to etch his plate in such a way that a good print could be made from it by any competent printer. His emphasis was on line and he did not rely on manipulating the inking of the plate to obtain his effect.

THE 1890 GENERATION

By the 1890 generation, we mean artists who were in their twenties in 1890, and were beginning to work at that time. For there was a definite 1890 generation, just as there was a 1660 and an 1830 generation. The year 1890 witnessed profound changes in taste and in all the arts.

By this time, the old professional engravers, the pupils of Henriquel-Dupont, had virtually stopped working or at any rate no longer counted. Goupil disappeared, and with him his type of engraving, which was becoming more and more commercial. On the other hand collectors were rapidly growing tired of etchings, and the fashion for them among society people died out, leading as we have already noted, to the bankruptcy of Cadart's widow. The print making of this period, or at least the print making which seems of any value to us, was done solely by painters and no longer by engravers. These painters found line engraving too exacting and disliked the uncertainty of etching; they preferred lithography to all other techniques. Being painters, they were not satisfied with black and white lithography. So following the example of the poster-artists (and some of the painters were poster-artists themselves) they took to colour lithography.

Toulouse-Lautrec was one of the masters of lithography. In 1893 L'Estampe Originale published an album of lithographs, *Le Café Concert,* with text by Georges Montorgueil containing eleven lithographs by Lautrec and the same number by Henri-Gabriel Ibels. Lautrec's subjects included Jane Avril, Yvette Guilbert, Aristide Bruant and Caudieux. During the 1890s Steinlen, Chévet and Jean-Louis Forain all produced magnificent work in the medium.

LITHOGRAPHY: THE NABIS

These lithographers formed a group round a leading publisher, Ambroise Vollard. In an unassuming shop in the rue Laffitte, Vollard assembled Vuillard, Denis, Roussel and Bonnard and started publishing their works from 1890 onwards. Later, he added those of Carrière, Degas, Renoir and Cézanne, but he remained attached to the first group in particular, and these are the ones who are of greater concern to us.

Vollard published these engravings partly because he was an intelligent speculator, partly because he liked prints. He published two albums of original engravings; the first, an edition of a hundred copies at a hundred francs each, contained twenty-nine prints in colour: two plates of *Bathers* by Cézanne, Lautrec's *la Charrette anglaise,* plates by Redon, Denis, Bonnard, Vuillard and Sisley; the second, in 1897, comprised thirty-two plates in black and white by Whistler, Besnard, Carrière, Redon, Munch and Puvis de Chavannes. A third appeared in 1900.

Among Vollard's group, Bonnard, Vuillard and Denis were in the vanguard: Bonnard with his famous poster, *France-Champagne,* in 1889, the first poster by a painter, his posters and book-jackets for Vollard, followed by his *Some Aspects of Paris Life* (twelve colour plates, 1899) and a folding screen (with a hundred and ten copies printed by Moline, also in 1897). Claude Roger-Marx rightly emphasizes the density of Bonnard's page setting, his use of light, and his 'subtle art of correspondence, of dynamic interaction of rhythms and colours.' Vuillard had at least as much talent as Bonnard: he began with black and white lithography, play-bills for the *Théâtre de l'Oeuvre,* then started doing colour lithography for Vollard from 1896, in particular for his *Paysages et Intérieurs* late in 1899 (printed by Clot). Another great painter lithographer was Maurice Denis, the author of the famous series *Amour* in 1899.

This type of lithography was to conquer a public for the Nabis (the name, from the Hebrew, means 'prophets'), and thanks to it, their art was to become widely known: their posters were to cover the walls of Paris, and their lithographs to hang in middle-class homes. When in 1924, Roger-Marx asked Bonnard why he had taken up engraving, the latter replied that he had had 'the idea of a popular art which would have new applications: engravings, furniture, fans, screens'. The intention is therefore explicit. The contribution of Marty and Henri Nocq to the realization of this vision was of great importance; Nocq opened a shop, *l'Artisan Moderne,* which produced and sold works of art at low prices, and Marty dealt in modern design for people of small means, publishing pamphlets on the *Musée du Soir* in working-class districts. It was not mere chance that Lautrec designed a poster for Nocq and that Bonnard worked for Marty. (England already had the Century Guild, founded in London as early as 1882, to bring together artists and designers.)

A link may be seen between the Nabis and Art Nouveau; a link with Henri Van de Velde (1863–1937), creator of the famous embossed wall-paper in 1891 and artistic adviser on numerous books and periodicals, and with Grasset's posters of 1896. The Nabis also played an important part in the renewal of book illustration. Illustration in France, although in great demand from 1870 on, had remained narrowly traditional. Maurice Leloir and his pupils had flooded the market with books whose pictures were based on the researches of Meissonier or on photographs, and were intended to be accurate representations of costumes and poses, past or present, without any attempt at artistic expression or effect. Moreover book-collectors, who were formed into powerful associations, considered their books merely as valuable *objects* to be treated with extreme care. Jules Renard made fun of them, writing in 1900: 'These men who know that one must turn the pages of a beautiful book by the top, and who always have both hands ready in case you let fall the book they are presenting for your admiration.'

Publishers were in search of a new form. After putting pictures between the pages of the text, technically the easiest method, they inserted pictures in the text in an attempt at a new style of layout. One rather unusual method was tried: changing the illustrations for each client. In 1892, the *Bibliophiles Contemporains* published an edition of Maupassant's *Contes* in which 'each member could have the margins of his copy decorated with original drawings by the artists of his choice'. Henri de Sta and Henry Somm had built themselves a reputation with this type of illustration, which Lautrec himself contemplated for a little (he started illustrating in water-colours the margins of *la Fille Elisa*). But the taste of the bibliophiles was still uncertain. Camille Pissarro, in 1891, had been invited to admire the collection of the most famous of them, Gallimard, and had been surprised at finding a Verlaine illustrated by Rodin in a binding painted in gouache by the modest Raphaëlli. That is why books illustrated by such painters as Bonnard, Denis and Lautrec created such a stir during the years 1893 to 1899, and created a new type of book. As Pascal Pia remarked, an important place must be granted to André Gide's *le Voyage d'Urien*, illustrated by Maurice Denis. This book, published in 1893, when the author was twenty-one and the illustrator twenty-three, does great credit to the bookseller Bailly who published it.

W. R. SICKERT. *'That Old Fashioned Mother of Mine'*. 1928. Etching

In 1899, Floury was bold enough to follow suit by asking Lautrec to illustrate Jules Renard's *Histoires Naturelles*. This marvellous book, whose text and illustrations complement each other to perfection, failed to sell. In 1900, Vollard himself took up the formula with Verlaine's *Parallèlement*, illustrated by Bonnard in pale red chalk, a book of very large format which needed to be placed on a lectern. Bonnard also illustrated for him *Daphnis and Chloé* in 1901, a book comprising 160 lithographs in grey and purplish-blue. Illustration in the archaeological sense was finished; no longer was it a màtter of monuments in the antique manner but of evocative touches and suggestions, in the same manner as the artist's paintings. Maurice Denis also worked for Vollard, who in 1911 published Verlaine's *Sagesse* with his illustrations. Denis had had this work in mind since 1890, and had shown Verlaine his sketches, but for a long time Vollard had hesitated to do such a book. In 1890 Denis had defined the spirit of his illustrations by a statement which was to mark an epoch: 'One can recognize intensity of expression in distorted drawings and smudges, and on the other hand weakness in drawings where the literary spirit introduces external elements.' Denis was also fascinated by the book as an end in itself; he had decided to do without a black border round the illustrations in the text and without the random cutting up of the text by illustrations, as practiced by his contemporaries.

Vollard may have guessed that this group was destined to succeed when he saw the success of the master of them all, Toulouse-Lautrec, who took up lithography in 1892 and revolutionized it with his broad touches in the manner of Hokusai and the Japanese print makers. With hasty, nervous outlines over which he applied vivid touches of colour, Lautrec's vigour and novelty created a sensation.

He may have been thinking of Whistler, who was also doing colour lithography at that time. Joseph Pennell has explained that he proceeded not by superimposing colours, as was done at the time, but by juxtaposing them. As many transfers would be made as there were colours, using a different stone for each colour. Then on each stone all but the areas to be printed in one colour would be scraped or etched away. Whistler prided himself on his original ideas, on his fondness of experiment, and on trying to rediscover the techniques of mixing and printing colours which gave the Japanese woodcuts their fresh and vivid colours. He expressed his 'horror' of coloured

PIERRE BONNARD. *The Costermonger*. 1897. Lithograph

copperplate engraving which he called 'abominable, vulgar and stupid' because the colour was applied with a pad and because the printing process ruined the drawing and destroyed the freshness of the colours. If we lay particular stress on Whistler, it is because of his important influence on both French and English print making, a point which has not received due attention.

But he had to overcome a great deal of opposition: at that time, colour lithographs were considered simply as broadsheets, and serious critics, as late as 1897, still denied all colour printing the right to a place in collectors' portfolios or in albums of prints. They were not entirely wrong since they did not know of the painters' lithographs we have just mentioned, but only of the chromo-lithographs which were flooding the market. We must remember that Vollard's books and experiments had not reached the general public.

These chromo-lithographs, executed by artists now forgotten, were widely bought and unfortunately played a prominent part in the everyday life of the time, in the form of calendars and greeting cards (the latter originated in America in 1873, the first being an imitation by a Mrs O. W. Whitney of the business card of the lithographer Louis Prang). Moreover, Vollard's team of painters did not persist later than 1900; after this date, lithography, particularly colour lithography, was little practised.'

THE WOODCUT: GAUGUIN

In the meantime, wood engraving was being radically transformed, no doubt because it was also practised by painters, and no longer by professional wood engravers alone. Suddenly the head of the professional engravers himself, Auguste Lepère, the apostle of the tone block, changed his point of view. He had done with reproductions and facsimiles, and turned to the German primitives and old French masters. But he kept his new style to himself for some time in order to earn a living. To Pissarro who came to visit him in 1885, Lepère explained how superior the old wood engravings were to those of the nineteenth century: 'Above all, do not make the mistakes we made; if we were to change our style, we would die of hunger, but you who do not yet know corruption, beware of it!' Indeed, a little later on, Lepère engraved a view of *Rouen Cathedral* (1888), which is the masterpiece of tone engraving. He was agitating among his friends; after Pissarro he gave a sermon to Joyau and then to Bracquemond; they were moved by his eloquence. Joyau made a note of the following: 'In a little lecture he read us last Saturday at Béraldi's, Lepère spoke words to this effect: With copper plates you get a delicate, light touch; with wood, which is matchless, vigour, strong oppositions of light and shade, etc. . . . This made me jibe inwardly. I am toiling and moiling precisely at giving wood suppleness and lightness, and going over his words,

I find a lot which is wrong and too violently and absolutely restricting; and something tells me, over-sensitive fool . . . that between the tameness of the tone block and the brutality of the woodcut, there is room for something else which is just what I am seeking to express.' Bracquemond, his friend and colleague, who enjoyed writing, and who was acquiring an audience among book-collectors, congratulated him. 'Wood should be used as wood,' he wrote in 1897, 'and not in imitation of copper plates or of photography.' One should, he added, draw directly on the wood with a pen or a pencil, and Lepère was quite right to reject tones, cuttings and overcuttings in favour of engraving with indentations in the early German manner. And one fine day, Lepère gave up reproduction wood-engraving for woodcuts, boldly and simply cut with a pen-knife. But a far more important master had preceded him: Gauguin.

Gauguin started engraving in 1889, but here we shall study neither his lithographs on zinc nor his first etchings (his portrait of Mallarmé in 1891). We shall only consider his woodcuts because they are the origin of the modern woodcut.

Gauguin made the first in Tahiti in 1892–3. He had arrived with an assortment of gouges and wood-sculptor's chisels. He had at once tried to get hold of some wood. He also tried to find engravings done by the natives, which probably never existed, although he insisted they did on the evidence of photographs he produced, showing the Marquesas islanders beautifully tattooed. He was surprised that artists capable of tattooing such images could have never thought of reproducing them on wood or stone. He himself tried his skill at it, and this was how his first woodcuts were done; one of them, *Maruru*, certainly dates from that period, as well as a whole series, among which are *Noa Noa* and *Nave Nave Fenua*. He pulled them himself with great difficulty in Tahiti, then had them printed in Paris, in colour, by Lucien Roy. Gauguin valued his woodcuts highly and was disappointed when they did not sell successfully in Paris in 1895. They were printed again in black and white after the 1914 War, and especially between 1921 and 1927, which explains their influence at that time.

In one of his letters, dated 1901, Gauguin explained these rough and original engravings, done without sophisticated techniques, but full of a wild poetry: 'The great mistake was Greek art, no matter how beautiful it was.' 'The vital sap is always present in primitive art, but not so, I think, in the arts

MAURICE DENIS. Jacket for *Douze lithographies d'Amour*. 1898. Lithograph

FRANCIS DODD. *Belvedere Road S.E.* Drypoint

of civilization at its height', and also: 'It is precisely because my engraving
returns to the primitive days of engraving that it is interesting: wood
engraving has become sickening . . . I am sure a time will come when these
woodcuts, so different from what is now being done, will be valuable.'
Indeed, the restraint and the density of his art as an engraver are quite
remarkable.

Gauguin also did woodcuts during his second stay in Tahiti. These are
perhaps less important, being mainly engraved after primitive sculptures,
but they became known to the Nabis who imitated them.

Gauguin was not alone in praising primitive art and the naiveté of the
ancients. Similar ideas were made fashionable by the author of *Ubu roi*,
Alfred Jarry (1873–1907), who attached great importance to *images* and
'honoured' them, according to J. Loise, as manifestations of reality. He owned
popular prints, poorly printed and gaudy, to which he ascribed an essential
role; he publicized them widely, saying that imitation of them would give
birth to modern wood engraving. There were reproductions of ancient wood

29

AUGUSTE LEPÈRE. *The Game of Backgammon.* 1891. Wood engraving

engravings in *Les Minutes de sable immémorial* (1894). *L'Imagier,* a review
edited by Jarry and Rémy de Gourmont from 1894 until they fell out with one
another in 1896, known as the 'Print Review', boldly mixed wood blocks by
Filiger, Emile Bernard, Jarry and Espagnat and a lithograph by the Douanier
Rousseau with reprints of works by Georgin and other popular prints. In the
same vein, its successor *Perinderion* (1896), which only lasted two numbers,
even reproduced pages on the monsters of the Munster *Cosmography*
(*circa* 1594), together with Dürers, Georgins, Emile Bernard, and a copper plate
from an old fencing manual.

Probably encouraged by Bonnard, Jarry also did a few lithographs and
woodcuts. (The woodcuts were inspired by the well-known gingerbread
figures of Dinan, and were signed Alain Jans.)

Emile Bernard also did woodcuts, imitating early white-line engraving.
But in 1897, Beltrand, who was to become Maurice Denis' printer, produced

30

PAUL GAUGUIN. *Te Atua (The Gods)*. 1895–1903. Woodcut

an almanac with colour woodcuts printed in water-colour in the Japanese style.

The years 1894–5 marked the renewal of English wood engraving with William Nicholson (1872–1949), who also worked with James Pryde as the Beggarstaff brothers. A little earlier, William Morris had founded the *Kelmscott Press* in Hammersmith, which was to publish, up to 1898, fifty-three books engraved on wood in the Pre-Raphaelite spirit. In London in 1894, Lucien Pissarro founded the *Eragny Press,* which functioned up to 1914, publishing books illustrated with colour wood engravings. Charles Ricketts (1866–1931), co-founder with C. H. Shannon of the *Vale Press,* also published books illustrated in a broad, unadorned style. Fine books illustrated by some of the best contemporary engravers were published by the Golden Cockerell Press, which more recently has been emulated by the Folio Society.

ENSOR, REDON AND THE FANTASTIC

During the same period, but using different techniques—etching and lithography—James Ensor and Odilon Redon expressed strange visions, dreams in which humanity was distorted. This way of seeing the world was not at all peculiar to art, since it was also expressed in the literature of the end of the nineteenth century.

Around 1886 and especially towards 1890, Ensor, who was twenty-six and who had been painting since the age of fifteen, took up print making; he discovered he had a taste for etching, doing some impressionist landscapes, but working mainly in the fantastic manner of his paintings, some of which (e.g. *The Cathedral*), he reproduced. 'In certain of his etchings, whether in colour or not, the artist of the fantastic comes to the fore—an artist shrinking neither from the wildest dreams nor from Rabelaisian salt, coarse salt, even sometimes cooking salt', Pol de Mont wrote of him in 1895. Those monsters, those *demons plaguing me,* those *scandalized masks,* that *skeletal portrait* have an extreme originality. The public and the critics were frightened and hostile, but Ensor protested his truthfulness and his sincerity. 'My century is like that,' he said, 'I have painted it as I have found it.' Indeed he found life hard and hostile; he lived in a solitude populated with monsters; in the words of Gusman, 'in daily converse with the dust-covered wreckage of existence

ALFRED JARRY. *Ubu roi.* C 1896–8. Woodcut

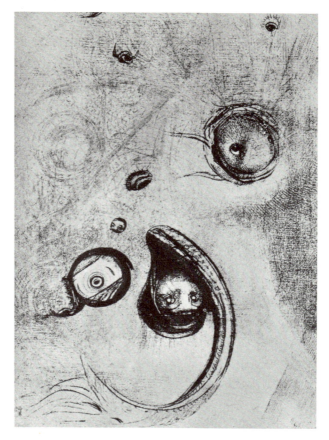

ODILON REDON. *'Et que des yeux sans tête flottaient comme des mollusques'.*
1896. Lithograph

and past splendour.' This unknown artist was to be discovered by a country
he did not like, France; in 1899 the young Paris review *La Plume* devoted a
special issue and an exhibition to him; Lautrec admired his masks.

Ensor was Redon's contemporary, and it was perhaps not by chance that
the first catalogue of Redon's works, by Jules Destrée, had been published in
Brussels around 1890. Redon, like Ensor, was a hallucinated artist. 'Everything happens,' he wrote, 'by surrender and the unconscious.' He was

ODILON REDON. *L'Art céleste*. 1894. Lithograph

obsessed by 'the dark world of the undefined'. Béraldi, like his contemporaries, found it difficult to understand these 'unintelligible hallucinations which have no meaning; it is black for the sake of black and white for the sake of white', is how he judged the famous series of lithographs by Redon, *Dans le Rêve* (1879), *A. Edgar Poe* (1882), and *La Tentation de saint Antoine* (1899), whose beauty and depth our own century has been able to appreciate. Huysmans, however, had admired prints by Redon in an exhibition at the daily newspaper *Le Gaulois* in 1882: 'He seems to have been musing upon

Poe's comforting aphorism: the only certainty is in dreams.' In 1890, Arthur Symons had called him the French Blake. As for Mallarmé, he thanked him in these words: 'You wave in our silences the plumage of dreams and the night. It all fascinates me, and most of all, that it should originate from your dreams alone. Invention has depths equal to certain blacks; lithographer and demon as you know you are, Redon, I envy you your world of myth.'

Degas' opinion, as reported by Thadée Natanson, was less studied: 'I do not understand much of what he means, but as for his blacks, oh, those blacks, to print finer ones would be impossible.'

JAMES ENSOR. *Musiciens fantastiques*. 1888. Etching

EDVARD MUNCH. *The Kiss*. 1905. Woodcut

During the same period, in 1895, Munch was doing his first woodcuts in Paris. Born in Norway in 1863, he soon decided to take up painting. He exhibited as early as 1881. In 1885, thanks to the painter Thaulow, Gauguin's brother-in-law, a lover of Paris, he was able to make a three-week stay in France. In 1889, he was given a three-year travel grant by the Norwegian government. Through Theo Van Gogh, he discovered the works of Vincent, and came under the influence of Gauguin and Lautrec; he got to know Fénéon and the *Théâtre de l'Oeuvre*. On returning home he had an exhibition in Oslo, which was a *succès de scandale,* then in Berlin in November 1892, where his paintings created a sensation. There he met the playwright Strindberg, and Meier-Graefe, the German historian of the Impressionists, a print enthusiast and publisher of lithographs whom he would meet again in Paris in 1895–8. He exhibited at the gallery of Bing, whose assistant Meier-Graefe was, then at the *Indépendants.*

Between 1898 and 1908 he worked in Germany, then returned to Norway where he had a nervous breakdown. As early as 1912 he was acclaimed in Cologne, where one exhibition devoted a whole room to his work, giving it a prominence equal to Cézanne's. His work had come to an end before 1916, but he lived alone and sick until 1944, having refused to be a member of the Council for Culture under the Occupation.

Two things influenced him profoundly: his immense pity for human suffering, and his admiration for the Nabis during his stay in Paris. His father was a doctor among the poor in Christiania, and Munch as a youth had accompanied him on his rounds; he could not forget the scenes of distress he saw. He discovered his personal mode of expression in Paris when he saw the Nabis. He said this himself, asserting that he owed more to France than to Germany. Love, death and despair were his habitual themes.

He enjoyed engraving; if he did not do more, it was because of the social message of his art, which he thought he could impress on a larger audience through painting. S. Willcock has told how, in Berlin in 1894, he first did rapid drypoints in the street and in coffee houses, and how much he admired the etchings of Manet. In Paris in 1896, he did his first woodcuts (Meier-Graefe had published a portfolio with eight of his prints in 1895), and exhibited them at Bing's. He was friendly with the Mollards, who showed him the experi-

EDVARD MUNCH. *Portrait of August Strindberg.* 1896. Lithograph

mental woodcuts which Gauguin had entrusted to them before leaving for Tahiti. In Paris he also did lithographs, inspired by Lautrec (for he had a copy of Lautrec's album *Elles,* which reinforced his own bitter view of women). Munch however is far from being a mere follower. His *The Cry* in 1895, his

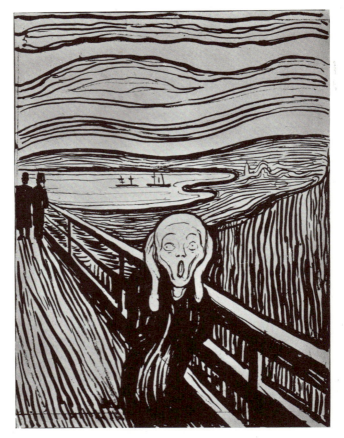

EDVARD MUNCH. *The Cry*. 1895. Woodcut, retouched print

Portrait of Mallarmé in 1896, his play-bill of Ibsen's *Peer Gynt* for the
Théâtre de l'Oeuvre also in 1896 are of unparalleled originality and violence.
Thadée Natanson devoted an article to him in November 1895 in the *Revue
Blanche,* the mouthpiece of the Nabis.

As Jean Cassou says, if you do not know Munch, you cannot understand
Expressionism; Munch's reputation is particularly high in Germany and in
the United States where he has been championed since 1912 by Neumann.
He is very much admired in Norway but his prints do not come on the market
there, for they were not a commercial success when they first appeared.

EDVARD MUNCH. *Anguish*. 1896. Woodcut

He stored them in large quantities and bequeathed his entire studio to the Norwegian State in 1940.

DEGAS

Etching seemed to be the domain of specialists, of 'cooks' like Buhot whom we have mentioned in the pages devoted to the previous generation. However, as with lithography and as with wood engraving, it was also practised by painters, and especially by Degas. Degas had started etching much earlier;

EDVARD MUNCH. *Peer Gynt*. 1896. Lithograph

he loved etchings, and he collected those of Manet and his friends; he wrote around 1878: 'I can think of nothing but etching, but I don't do any.' If he did not, it was precisely because he did not dare show the modern etchings he wanted to do next to those of Buhot, which were so admired. Now, he had come across Renoir at Cadart's around 1890, and seeing his etchings, he had

42

said: 'There are always experts to say that it looks as if it were done any old how, and by somebody who knows nothing of the rules: but how beautiful it is.' This sentence is revealing; it is a recognition of the idea of the artist's print, and Degas was to put this into practice with his *Laundresses* and his *After the Bath*. He exhibited in 1889 at the *Peintres Graveurs*, where Mallarmé pointed out to Berthe Morisot 'some exquisite trifles', these trifles being artists' prints.

THE HUMOROUS JOURNALS

With Munch and Degas, we saw the birth of Expressionism; before we examine its effect on print making, particularly in Germany, let us briefly trace its origins. They can be found in the drawings in humorous journals, whose influence has never been adequately stressed. We need not dwell on the great ancestor, Daumier, whose drawings for *Charivari* have been admired by several generations, and whose lithographs Degas collected; nor on André Gill, whose caricatures printed in *l'Eclipse,* with their oversized heads, started a trend which has lasted to this day (Gill died insane in 1885, but Courteline praised him in 1883, and in 1895 his bust was placed at the top of the rue des Martyrs in Montmartre). The magazine *le Rire* was founded in 1894 by Arsène Alexandre, the biographer of Daumier, and Lautrec contributed to it as early as 1896. *Simplicissimus* of Munich was founded in 1896 by the excellent German caricaturist Thomas Theodor Heine, who had worked for the newspapers since 1889. Among its contributors were Paul Bruno and Kandinsky. Caricature was spreading; papers had their own caricaturists, such as Caran d'Ache of the *Figaro,* who was very much influenced by Burch and Oberlander (a fact which he both admitted and regretted). Caricature also entered the world of literature; Jules Renard, an admirer of Lautrec, wrote in 1891, 'It is surprising how much these literary celebrities are improved by being seen as caricatures.' Renard's *Journal* contained some epigrammatic phrases, which might well be used as captions for caricatures: 'I must come and see you tomorrow to tell you my troubles; then there will be two people with troubles instead of one.' Though a friend of the humorous writers Alphonse Allais, Tristan Bernard and Alfred Capus, he affected to scorn

OLAF GULBRANSSON. *Simplicissimus.* 1908. Line and half-tone reproduction of
pen and wash drawing

FÉLIX VALLOTTON. *Lalique's Shop-window*. 1901. Woodcut

humorists: 'A humorist is a man who stands wide-eyed. He understands nothing of life, and gazes on it fascinated.'

Another friend of Renard's was Forain, who started his career in the humorous journals, but won recognition around 1887, after joining the *Courrier Français*. Some of his contemporaries placed him even higher than Degas. Bayard wrote in 1900 that 'compared with Degas' stupefied creatures, what Forain shows us is a veritable magic lantern'. J. Lethève, who made a thorough study of his work and drew up the first catalogue of it, recognized his incisive talent as that of the 'creator of modern caricature' which was drawn for the newspapers and expressed everything in a few lines ('very good,' de Rodys said in the *Figaro*, 'but too much white in your compositions'), but he disapproved of the grating wit which the Dreyfus affair inspired in Forain. The conciseness and power of his famous captions (people said he should have entered the Académie française rather than the Académie des Beaux-Arts), followed that of his drawing; the editors of the papers he worked for tended to recoil from their violence, so he would exaggerate them on his first draft. Thus, to be allowed to write the word *unscrupulous,* he would put *blackguard,* which his editor, Calmette, then corrected to *dishonest.*

Hermann-Paul (1864–1940), though less well-known than Forain, was an artist of great talent. In 1890 he worked with Vuillard, whose influence can be recognized in his *scènes de moeurs,* done in the manner of the Nabis, which appeared in the *Courrier français* from 1894 on. He influenced the German Thomas Theodor Heine (1867–1948), who started doing his *Simplicissimus* sketches about 1896, and was also inspired by Caran d'Ache. The most interesting caricaturist outside France at this time, and the most talented, was the Norwegian Olaf Gulbransson (1873–1958), who worked in Oslo and Munich after a stay in Paris in 1900. Klee would have liked to work for *Simplicissimus,* but his drawings were rejected in 1906.

The year 1894 saw the appearance of Vallotton's *Paris intense.* A Swiss artist who came to Paris in 1882 at the age of seventeen, he worked for a long time for fashion magazines, before finding his true medium in wood engraving in 1891, as seen in a still rather awkward work, *l'Enterrement.* In 1892 he did *les Nécrophores,* in 1893, *le Mauvais pas des porteurs de cercueil dans l'escalier,* in 1894, *l'Exécution.* The titles alone show the morbid and macabre side of this 'neo-xylographer' as Octave Uzanne called him. He purposely stressed this side of himself by such a lavish use of black that his friends used to say he was always engraving 'funeral cards'. ('Vallotton did a daring thing: he clearly opposed white surfaces to flat black surfaces, without hatching or trickery of any kind', Avermaete noted). Soon he was treating social subjects; his *Paris intense,* a series of very dark lithographs printed from prepared zinc plates on canary yellow paper, were reminiscent of Vuillard, but with strong emphasis on the faces; the series depicts gatherings, revolutionary scenes, an accident and scenes in the rain. His restrained sensuousness gave birth to another series, of ten wood engravings, very black —too black in fact—printed on cream-coloured paper, entitled *Intimités,* and published by the *Revue Blanche* in 1898.

AUBREY BEARDSLEY. *The Wagnerites. C* 1895. Indian ink drawing

PAUL-CÉSAR HELLEU. *The Duchess of Marlborough. C* 1901. Drypoint

THE AESTHETES: HELLEU, BEARDSLEY

The 1900s, more so perhaps than the 1890s, was a decade of aesthetes. Indeed, the aesthetic movement, born with Huysmans' *A Rebours,* had finally reached the general public, which greeted Helleu and Beardsley with enthusiasm.

Helleu started etching in 1885. His friend, the painter Tissot, encouraged him and gave him a diamond point, much finer than the steel points generally used by his contemporaries for their drypoints; he stopped etching about

PABLO PICASSO. *Woman's Head, Profile*. 1905. Drypoint on copper

1921. His two best periods were about 1893 and 1899. Helleu's art cannot be separated from his life or from his period.

His most famous drypoint was the portrait of the Duchess of Marlborough, of which nearly a thousand copies were printed; seven hundred were sold at once, at 100 francs each. He followed this with several other portraits of the Duchess and her beautiful contemporaries. Helleu is important not only from an aesthetic but also from a historical point of view, for his drypoints of women of fashion spread the vogue for a certain type of woman: the tall, slim Parisienne.

49

Aubrey Beardsley (1872–98), who died at twenty-six, worked less than eight years, starting in 1891. He combined the perversity of a Félicien Rops with the faces and elongated bodies of Rossetti's figures; we see this particularly in Beardsley's illustrations in the *Yellow Book* and Oscar Wilde's *Salome,* and in his drawings in the *Courrier français*. Jacques-Emile Blanche, who knew him well in Dieppe, wrote in 1907 that he was par excellence a graphic artist: 'The heraldic engraver and the medieval image-maker lend the exactness of their art to the young *decadent*. He is a master in *white and black*. His drawings are posters ready to hang on the walls of London: are not illustrations and posters the very art of our times?' Beardsley was immediately well received in England 'and in the new French school'. In 1893 Pennell, who owned the drawing for the *Wagnerites,* published the first article about him in *The Studio,* a magazine with a large following. Beardsley was to have a great influence up to 1914, and Paul Klee, who studied him in the Munich Print Room, wrote: 'his style is provocative and gives food for thought'.

Beardsley's most significant work is the Indian ink drawing *The Wagnerites,* reproduced in volume 3 of the *Yellow Book,* which dates from the period when fashionable intellectuals all went to hear *Tristan* or *The Valkyrie.*

KLEE AND PICASSO, 1903–5

In 1903 Paul Klee made a print to which he always gave a very important place in his work, and which he printed in three states. This was the *Comedian*: a comedian with a tragic face, half hidden behind the mask of a comic character of the antique theatre. Klee explained this already explicit work on several occasions; he stressed the idea of the mask: a work of art behind which the man is seen. It is a striking work; its grandeur, its slightly naive feeling and the fineness of its technique make it an outstanding one. Yet Klee was aware that he lacked technical training; he made attempts at zinc etching and glass plates, but he claimed he dared not continue beyond one series of prints 'because I am not a specialist'. In 1905 he regarded his engravings, in musical language, as 'my first complete opus'. He wanted to go further, for 'what has been recorded ceases to live'. The public did not encourage him in

PABLO PICASSO. *The Frugal Meal*. 1904. Zinc etching

PABLO PICASSO. *Salome.* 1905. Drypoint on copper

PABLO PICASSO. *The Acrobats*. 1905. Drypoint on copper

this direction, and he expressed his disappointment in his diary. His prints were first rejected by the publisher Cassirer, then by the Berlin galleries, and when he was finally able to exhibit them in Munich in 1906, they hardly received a mention.

1904 is the year of Picasso's *Frugal Meal*. Picasso, who is to play a key part three or four times in this book, appears here for the first time. As for other

JEAN-EMILE LABOUREUR. *Portrait of Henri de Toulouse-Lautrec.* 1906. Woodcut

great artists, such as Segonzac, for Picasso prints are not merely a diversion, but a particular mode of expression, at least as valid as painting. For years, he gave himself to print making to the exclusion of any other form. From that point of view, he is in the tradition of Meryon, Rembrandt and Daumier, not that of Degas or Manet, who did indeed produce printed masterpieces, but did not follow them up.

What did print making mean to him and why does he work the way he does? It is no use asking him, since Sabartes tells us: 'He does not like to give his opinion, he hates giving interviews'. Let us then watch him at work. He does not work to fill an order, to please a publisher or a client, but above all because he has a passion for graphics. He says so himself. When in 1946 he visited an exhibition of children's drawings organized in Paris by the British Council, on seeing those naive splashes of colour, he said: 'As a child I could not have taken part in an exhibition like this, for at the age of twelve I was drawing like Raphael.' There are many examples that show his devotion to drawing, among them the story that he liked to teach the Montmartre urchins how to draw on the sand with one uninterrupted stroke. Gertrude Stein stressed the fact that lines were for him 'more important than anything', and she called to mind elsewhere the 'calligraphic quality' of Picasso's work. The fact that he is a great draughtsman explains his prints: with very few exceptions they are not works of skilful appearance, not *finished* works, with hatching effects, but works in which the arabesque takes up more and more space, in which the lines become increasingly important. He himself insisted on his dislike of *finished* work: 'To finish means to have done with an object, to kill it, to give it the *puntilla*, to dispatch it, to deal it the finishing stroke.'

A series of central importance is the one composed of seventeen etchings done in 1904–5. Picasso had then decided to stay in Paris; it was the end of his blue period, he had settled down in Montmartre at the famous 'Bateau-lavoir' in the place Ravignan. He was leading a very difficult life, sustained by the friendship of Apollinaire, Max Jacob and André Salmon. The last, in his *Négresse du Sacré-Coeur* (1920), depicted him in the guise of Sorgue, hurling 'into an eccentric inferno a leprous and imploring humanity'. Indeed the *Acrobats* and the *Beggars* studied from life in Montmartre were his favourite models. He also saw, in Paris itself, the gipsies and beggars that Nouel y Monturiol (1873–1911) painted. Having painted them, he tried

OSCAR KOKOSCHKA. *Bookplate: les garçons rêveurs* 1908. Lithograph

his hand at etching them. He was at once successful.

The most famous is the one called *The Frugal Meal*. A thin, wretched man is stroking with his long, delicate hands the arms of a very beautiful woman with a strange expression on her face, but averting his marked, blind face with its terrible empty sockets which would shock her. The woman's gaze is also avoiding him and she is staring sadly into the distance. If one can speak of the poetry of a print it is certainly here, where intense, unformulated *sorrow* has a sublime greatness rarely equalled except in certain plates by Van Gogh or Munch. The human significance is very beautiful, with the man only wanting to give the woman his caresses, and averting from her things which could hurt or frighten her. Picasso engraved this masterpiece, for lack of a copper plate which he could not afford, on an already used zinc plate with a landscape still faintly visible. He was understandably very fond of it; he gave proofs to his best friends, and in his *Souvenirs* André Salmon tells us how he received one as a gift, and kept it lovingly, in spite of the pressures of financial difficulties and of Ambroise Vollard: 'The sideways glances the whimsical Vollard would cast on those two heart-rending poor people's figures, sitting at a table of affliction . . .' Fernande Olivier, the Master's companion, had seen him working on it, and she said how she had been struck by that half-starved couple from which 'emerged an intense expression of misery and alcoholism'.

Picasso had a few plates printed on fine paper by his neighbour, the printer Auguste Delâtre. The latter, who was soon to die at eighty-five, had printed first Meryon's etchings, then those of the etchers published by Cadart.

In the same series we admire other striking plates: two studies of women's heads of rare beauty, the plate called *les Pauvres*, and plates done in line, with strolling players practising, horses, the big acrobat at rest, of whom he also did a painting and a drawing, a daring *Salome* and three magnificent Harlequin prints. Picasso always treated etchings like drawings; he used his lack of technical experience and even the faults in his plates to make them into prints which are now classics. He worked alone and for himself, and his works remained unknown for a long time except by a few friends; it was not until 1913 that they were bought by Vollard who had them steel faced and a hundred copies printed.

This cult of the poor and destitute was the expression of the Picasso of

RAOUL DUFY. *La Havanaise*. 1904. Etching

that period, who having recently come to Paris from Barcelona, was living
in penury and despair among empty sardine tins and oyster shells. He was
driven to contemplate suicide by the incomprehension of the public ('What
fools!' he said, even in those early days), a public which in other parts of the
town and among other circles, was enjoying life to the full. André Germain,
director of the big bank, the Crédit Lyonnais, is moved when he recalls
those years: 'Dear 1906,' he writes, 'one of the few happy years of my tor-
mented life.' This was the year of the *dîner de têtes* with Maurice Barrès,

Madame de Noailles, Jacques-Emile Blanche and Paul Adam. But Picasso's *misérabilisme* has its roots in something deeper and more noble than sheer destitution. Antonina Valentin's excellent analysis points to his 'demoniacal attraction to what is ugly and evil' and to a deep feeling of loneliness, which gave rise to the themes of the couple taking refuge in love, and the outcasts of society. This latter theme is also to be found in the poems of his friend Apollinaire, of whom he was thinking when he said: 'I paint, and they write', and who worshipped his paintings for their nostalgic poetry. One of the poems in *Alcools* is called *les Saltimbanques* (wandering acrobats):

> 'Dans la plaine les baladins
> S'éloignent au long des chemins
> Devant l'huis des auberges grises
> Par les villages sans églises.'

And even closer to the *Frugal Meal*, Apollinaire, 'tired with this ancient world', and fond of the refreshing naiveté of hand-bills, posters and coarsely illustrated serialized thrillers, described Picasso:

> 'Tu es debout devant le zinc d'un bar crapuleux,
> Tu prends un café à deux sous parmi les malheureux.'

But in 1905, Picasso changed his style and his subjects. It was the beginning of the pink period, and he made no more prints for several years, until his cubist period.

EXPRESSIONISM

Between 1904 and 1907, Emil Nolde made his best prints—very striking and original works using different techniques. In 1937 he was judged by the Nazi government to be among the creators of degenerate art and the official celebrations for his seventieth birthday were cancelled; in 1941 he was expelled from the Reichkunstkammer and forbidden to work. After the war he was gloriously compensated, for before his death in 1956 he received the first prize at the Venice Biennale of 1950 for his graphic work.

Nolde was a solitary man. His real name was Hansen but he took the name of his native town after his marriage in 1901 at the age of thirty-four. Influenced by his peasant origin, by his fascination for primitive art (for a long time he dreamed of going to black Africa, and he finally did so in 1913), and by the works of Ensor (whom he did not meet until 1911), he went to Paris in 1900. His *Fantaisies* date from 1904, his wood engravings from 1906 and his lithographs from 1907 (his last etchings were done in 1922, his last lithographs in 1926). None of his prints brought him financial success, and he had to live by selling post-cards in water-colour after his drawings, thus earning enough to leave his teaching job in St Gallen. The first article about him came out as late as 1907, when he was forty. He was later a member of the *Brücke* and of the *Blaue Reiter* and fought against the *Secession* movement of Liebermann.

After the 1914 War, we see the development of the German Expressionist movement with Kirchner, Pechstein and Barlach, but it must be stressed that the movement started before the First World War, in particular with the *Brücke* (the bridge), whose first exhibition took place in Dresden in 1906. The origin of the movement is usually ascribed to the discovery by the Germans of Japanese prints, thanks to an exhibition of them in 1902, and of African sculpture, which was exhibited at the Ethnographical Museum in Dresden in 1903, as well as the influence of the review *Pan*. But it is very much more important to say that the movement is contemporary with Fauvism. However, no matter what the influences, a movement can only really exist if it is made up of very talented artists. This was so about 1906, when a certain number of innovating German artists gave new life to the art of the woodcut.

Among these was August Macke, who was not in fact able to give the best of his talent since he died in the First World War, and more importantly, Erich Heckel whose graphic work is considerable (close on 1,000 works). Heckel was very gifted, and between 1910 and 1913 he did excellent wood-cuts in black and white and in colour. His figures of naked women, his heads of thick-lipped Negro women, his entwined bodies, have a rare mixture of vigour and poetry. But Heckel could forget neither Gauguin nor the French *Fauves*.

ERICH HECKEL. *Self-portrait*. 1913. Woodcut

In 1912, *Der Blaue Reiter* came out in Munich, published by Piper, a kind of almanac containing drawings by children and the insane as well as ethnographical research. The publication was edited by Kandinsky, and followed an exhibition of graphic art by the group of the same name, which had taken

WASSILY KANDINSKY. *Composition*. 1906. Woodcut

place in April. The *Blaue Reiter's* almanac was the outcome of research done by Kandinsky and Franz Marc between 1906 and 1912. 'We invented the name in a coffee-house in Sindelsdorf. We all liked blue, Marc liked horses and we liked riders.' 'We were seeking,' wrote Marc in 1912, 'behind the mask of appearances, hidden things which we find more interesting than those discovered by the Impressionists.' Kandinsky who had published in Paris, from 1902 to 1904, colour woodcuts in the tradition of the French painters, close in spirit to the early works of Jacques Villon, became interested in Primitivism in 1906. He was forty-five and lived in Paris where he had previously stayed in 1889, 1892 and 1902. He exhibited at the Indépendants and the Salon d'Automne. He was more interested in Russian popular prints, than Gauguin's or Vallotton's woodcuts. We must not forget that he was actually artistic director of a printing firm in Moscow in 1895. He had his *Xylographies* (white-line engravings) published in Paris in the review *Tendances Nouvelles,* whose director asked him for another ten woodcuts in 1906. His primitivism is important if we compare it with that of, say, Archipenko, who came to Paris in 1908 to study 'archaic art' at the Louvre. When we next meet Kandinsky in 1922, he is making abstract prints, although his abstract paintings date back to 1910.

We must once more point out the divorce of the public from the artist. The public did not buy the *Blaue Reiter's* almanac, nor Kandinsky's *Xylographies*. The Print Rooms received copies of them but nobody referred to them at the time.

Two Mexican engravers must also be mentioned: the great maestro José Posada (1852–1913), and also Diego Riveira who came to Paris in the years 1906–8, and like so many others, was influenced by Gauguin.

ALBERTO MARTINI. *The Murders in the Rue Morgue.* 1907–8. Etching

UMBERTO BOCCIONI. *Beata solitudo—Sola beatitudo*. 1908. Etching

JUAN GRIS. *Income Tax*. 1908. Lithograph

FRANK BRANGWYN. *The Bridge.* 1904. Etching

*Though Juan Gris, like Jacques Villon, refused to acknowledge the drawings
he did for the illustrated papers, these drawings stand out from the mediocre
efforts of the professional illustrators, as do certain drawings by Galanis. One
such drawing by Gris is* Income Tax *('Give me twenty sous'. 'I haven't got that
much'. 'How many are you short?' 'Nineteen.') Draughtsmen were always
warmly welcomed by newspaper directors; Juveu for example, used to send out
a car to bring Villon to* le Rire. *Print makers were also pleased to obtain a larger
public than would have been possible had their work been confined to the
portfolios of the print dealers. This is why we are showing a few of these drawings,
which are not strictly speaking original prints.*

Contrary to what one might think, Cubism, a reaction against Impressionism, which was only just beginning to have some success, and also a reaction against Expressionism, was, as Picasso said, 'the will to find more expressive forms, to give more total forms to objects'. It appeared in painting before appearing in prints. This is how Kahnweiler explains the phenomenon: 'These painters had no intention of ending up doing futile calligraphy. They were realists, and the Cubist endeavour was precisely tending towards a more real figuration . . . From then on, it was the *essence* and not the appearance of objects that these painters wanted to render.' These graphic experiments, which were apparently going to fascinate twentieth-century engravers, and which had previously fascinated those of the seventeenth century, such as Bracelli, came after the corresponding experiments in painting. For Cubism began in painting: the first painting to be recognized as part of this new trend being Picasso's *The Young Ladies of Avignon* (1907). The year 1907 saw the birth of Cubism. This was the time of the discovery of Negro art and its carvings with their simplified forms, which some have considered as the 'incunabula' of Cubism. Indeed, there is no doubt that this sculpture influenced contemporary artists. But there was another great influence: Cézanne, who died in 1906 and who was given a very important retrospective exhibition in 1907. Picasso and Braque, in the first years of Cubism, produced works very much under the influence of Cézanne: the drawing is unadorned, the organization and composition are rigorous, there is no element of anecdote; the painting is restricted to design, form and colour.

In September 1908, Matisse, a member of the committee of the sixth Salon d'Automne which rejected Braque's entry and a composition by André Lhote, considered as too revolutionary, speaks for the first time of 'little cubes'. The term is taken up by Vauxcelles in the Journal *Gil Blas,* about Braque who 'disregards form, reduces everything—places, figures and houses—to geometrical forms, to cubes'. Kahnweiler ordered from Picasso the first cubist prints, the illustrations to Max Jacob's *Saint Matorel,* published in 1911. The etchings were done in 1910 at Cadaques. 'The cubist technique easily found its equivalent in engraving, the short brush-strokes of analytical cubism being replaced by clean lines or by points to create shadow and relief.' In 1912,

JACQUES VILLON. *Bal du Moulin Rouge.* 1910. Etching

Picasso did his second cubist print, his *Man with a dog,* Marcoussis did his *Portrait of Guillaume Apollinaire,* Braque his *Papier Job,* and in 1913, Jacques Villon his series on *Félix Barré* and the *Equilibristes.* Although the other three pieces preceded his, a fact which he never denied, Villon probably remains the standard model of cubist print making. Indeed, apart from the *Saint Matorel* which has the obvious value of a forerunner, Braque's works are variations on his paintings. Villon was the only one who etched for the sake of etching. He was a skilful etcher, who, born in 1875, had behind him a very large body of work as a draughtsman for illustrated journals (going back as far as 1894) and as a colour engraver (from 1900). When he was nearing forty, he turned his back on an easy success and a pleasant life, and for about thirty-five years, he waited in vain for recognition from a public slow to understand the value and the beauty of the *Portrait of Félix Barré,* of the famous *Equilibriste* and of *M. D. Reading.* After these masterpieces, his work was interrupted while he fought in the war, and he only started etching again in 1920. He achieved what he himself called Impressionist-Cubism, a form of Cubism which, after a few prints which excited great interest, returned to what François Stahly justly called *verisimilitude,* 'where the geometrical network of lines is linked only at a few vital points with the model provided by nature'. Turpin had realized at the time that Villon was an Impressionist Cubist, and he said: 'Jacques Villon has tinged Cubism with Impressionism, and with an almost scientific construction he has succeeded in paying his tribute at the same time to the human figure, to nature and to poetry.'

Robert Delaunay was also influenced by Cézanne between 1908 and 1910. It was at this period that he did his studies on the *Saint-Séverin* church and the Eiffel Tower. Delaunay used to call this Cubist period his 'destructive period': he was studying the 'dissolution of forms by light', and he later noted: 'Nothing is horizontal, nothing is vertical, light distorts everything, there is no longer any geometry.'

Juan Gris (1887–1927) did drawings for the humorous journals. It was he who did the cover of the first issue of *Purotania, journal des purotins,* in 1908; he also did drawings for *l'Assiette au beurre,* as did Kupka, from 1894. We must also mention Louis Marcoussis, who, from 1907, lived in Montparnasse and hated his work as a draughtsman for minor journals (*La Vie Parisienne, Mouche* in Cracow). In 1912, he did the cubist portrait of

29/30

JACQUES VILLON. *La Petite Mulâtresse*. 1911. Etching

ROBERT DELAUNAY. *Saint-Séverin*. 1926. Lithograph

Apollinaire, exhibited in the *Section d'Or* of 1912, and the portrait of *la Belle Martiniquaise*; his work was interrupted by the war, but he returned to print making after 1918.

One need hardly emphasize the feeling of gratitude behind the portrait of Apollinaire by Marcoussis, since Apollinaire had tried to define Cubism and win recognition for it: 'What differentiates Cubism from the old painting,' he was to write in 1913, 'is that it is not an art of imagination but an art of elevating a concept to the point of creation', and he assigned to cubist artists the mission of representing 'new structures from elements not taken from visual reality but created entirely by the artist, and endowed by him with a powerful reality of their own.'

In this same year, 1912, the press violently attacked the second Salon of the *Section d'Or*, founded the previous year by the *groupe de Puteaux,* which used to meet at Villon's and included Leger, La Fresnaye and Kupka among its members. The Salon d'Automne was also attacked. An open letter from a Monsieur Lampué to the Minister of Fine Arts, recommended him to visit the Salon d'Automne: 'You will see in this Salon the saddest display and accumulation of ugly and vulgar sights you can possibly imagine.'

In England, thanks to the critic Roger Fry, who consistently gave the movement his support, Cubism had made a tentative appearance in 1910 on the occasion of an exhibition devoted to 'Manet and the Post-Impressionists', where two works by Picasso were shown.

Cubist prints passed almost unnoticed. A few were shown at the Salon d'Automne of 1912–13, but it seems that they were practically unknown even to artists.

Nevertheless, the technique and subject-matter of prints had completely changed, thanks to Cubism. The general influence of the movement was undeniable. A great many artists joined the movement, but it did not remain the original Cubism following in the footsteps of Cézanne. Braque turned towards analytical Cubism (1910–12), Delaunay towards what was known as Orphism, others towards Abstraction. The influence of the movement went beyond France; as early as 1911, Berdaiev in Moscow was very much affected by a Picasso exhibition he saw at the Chukin Gallery; he expressed the pain he felt at the explosion and dematerialization of forms, and wrote these prophetic words: 'After Picasso and the cosmic wind which has swept over

LOUIS MARCOUSSIS. *Portrait of Guillaume Apollinaire*. 1912. Etching

painting, there can be no return to ideal beauty.' However, the reception of Cubist exhibitions by the general public was quite different. A drawing in the *Journal amusant* of 1909, by Luc, two caricatures of *Cubists* shown at the Salon des Humoristes in 1912, a caricature of a Cubist painting in *Le Sourire* of November 1912, and a drawing by Joseph Hémard of attendants removing

PABLO PICASSO. *The Man with the Guitar*. 1915. Line engraving

visitors to the 1912 Salon des Indépendants, who had been taken ill or gone insane, show the lack of understanding that existed on the part of the bourgeois public.

Cubism must be acknowledged as one of the most far-reaching aesthetic revolutions in the history of art. This is a notion which Apollinaire attempted to convey in his essay, *Méditations esthétiques—Les peintres Cubistes*, published in 1913. Another work of the period: *Du Cubisme* by Gleizes and Metzinger (1912), is important because it sanctions the name of Cubism, and is the first theoretical essay on the subject.

FUTURISM

This movement was heralded by a now famous manifesto by the painter and poet Marinetti, which appeared in the *Figaro* of 11 February 1909. This was followed by the so-called manifesto of the futurist painters in 1910, by a lecture by the painter Boccioni in Milan in March 1910, and by another lecture by Boccioni in Rome in 1911. In February 1912 there was an exhibition in Paris at the Bernheim Jeune gallery, prefaced by Boccioni, to whose ideas we are indebted in the paragraphs that follow.

The first idea was that of movement: 'Our ever-increasing desire for truth can no longer be satisfied with form and colour as they have been understood up to now. *Everything is moving*, running, rapidly changing. A profile is never still before us . . ., objects in movement multiply, change shape and pursue each other like vibrations.' The second idea was: 'We must paint what is new, *the fruits of our industrial age*'. 'Old walls, old palaces make me feel sick.' (Boccioni's *Diary*, 1907.)

The idea of movement lead the Futurists to extol distortion as an expression of life; this meant a struggle against the old culture, a conflict of particular importance in Italy, where the artists felt crushed by the weight of Antiquity and the Renaissance. The movement included several engravers: Boccioni, whose engravings are less curious than his paintings, except for a *Landscape* done in 1909 with industrial plant in the background; Rossolo (1885–1947) a painter and musician; and R. Romani, a lithographer. The movement however is even more interesting from the ideological point of view than for the works of art it produced. It did not survive the First World War. Boccioni, who was born in 1882, was in Paris from 1902 to 1908; he did an *Allegory of the Nativity* in the manner of Art Nouveau for the 1907 number of the *Illustrazione italiana*; in 1911 he returned to Paris, where he saw the works of the Cubists.

Severini, a friend of Max Jacob, Modigliani, Picasso and Braque, introduced Boccioni and his other Italian friends to them.

FAUVISM

It would be quite wrong to suppose that Cubism and Futurism were enjoying great success just before the First World War, even in artistic circles. Vlaminck, in his novel *Tournant dangereux*, shows that it was quite otherwise; in mid-June 1914, he saw aesthetes at the Paul Guillaume gallery fascinated by a 'Cubist outpouring' and their admiration gave him 'the presentiment of an abyss'. 'I saw the boundless stupidity of man. Suddenly, in a flash, I foresaw the war.' Indeed, Vlaminck, like Derain, had understood differently the necessity for a new outlook in art. *The Bridge at Cagnes* by Derain, about 1910, is one of the few Fauvist prints. Actually, it stands to reason that the explosion of colours in Fauvism is not particularly well served by print making, and it is all to the honour of Derain to have made this very successful attempt.

Dunoyer de Segonzac's *Dessins sur les danses d'Isadora Duncan,* and his album of twenty-four drawings on the theme of *Schéhérazade,* both of 1910, with their felicitous abbreviations and their astonishing feeling for rhythm and the dance, do not owe anything to Cubism.

Rouault owes nothing to Cubism either. While Villon was etching *le Petit Equilibriste,* Rouault was doing *le Miserere,* a series of fifty plates which Vollard published between 1922 and 1927, but which appeared only in 1948. These desperate and violent prints, showing hatred for all that is false, conventional and artificial, as well as an immense compassion, have had a considerable appeal for our day and age. But if we bear in mind that Rouault

JACQUES VILLON. *L'Equilibriste*. 1913. Drypoint

did them during the First World War, at the end of a happy era during which the middle classes behaved particularly selfishly, then the *Miserere* takes on its true significance.

Rouault, who was born in Paris during the Commune, learned to make stained glass before studying under Gustave Moreau. In 1906 he met Léon Bloy, and they later became friends. He liked Bloy's violence and his loathing for the bourgeoisie. But he went further than Bloy, who reproached him for his 'vertigo of ugliness'. His disgust for the world became even stronger when in 1908 he attended court hearings at the Palais de Justice, and was amazed to see the judges decide what was Good and what was Evil. He expressed himself through painting, but Vollard, who bought his studio in 1913, induced him to do prints. He liked black and white etchings, and said that 'with black and white, Forain kindled in me, child that I was, a glimmer, the essence of something rare which made me cling to hope'. Rouault has told how he began by making prints from drawings in Indian ink, and then painted pictures at Vollard's request which Vollard had transferred to copper plates, letting Rouault go on from there: 'I tried, with great pains, to preserve the original rhythm and outline. On each plate, I worked with various tools . . . But I was not satisfied, and I returned to the task again and again, doing as many as twelve or fifteen successive states.' An admirer of clowns, prostitutes, mountebanks, answering 'silently certain inner calls', he made this series his confession, for as he said, 'a work of art is a far more touching confession than can ever be spoken'. He worked for himself above all, and Vollard, with slight apprehension, let him do so: 'What an outcry will greet the *Miserere.*' It measured 26 by 20 inches. 'After all,' mused Vollard, 'the bibliophiles need only stand their Rouaults on choir stalls'.

In 1908, Maillol undertook to illustrate the *Eclogues* of Virgil for the great collector, Count Kessler. Maillol chose the text himself, and went to Greece to see the landscapes; he was enchanted by them, as he found a striking resemblance to Banyuls, where he was working. He was happy engraving and said that he was adding to his sculpture 'the love of books and graphic ornamentation'. On his walks, he would note down in a sketch-book a shape or an attitude, then do woodcuts; he did this for several years, from 1912 to 1914, and his volume came out as late as 1925. It was a particularly well

GEORGES ROUAULT. Lithograph from *Miserere*. 1922–3

finished book with special paper, special typography and studied page setting, and the woodcuts were said to have the beauty of bas-reliefs.

Maillol returned to book illustration much later, after 1935. Meanwhile, Cubism, Fauvism and Expressionism were each used in turn in a series of experiments with fashion plates, the experiments being those of the sumptuous couturier Paul Poiret. Poiret, who was a friend of painters such as Boussingault and Segonzac, and 'a pupil of Doucet and the Russian Ballets', wanted to renew the aesthetics of the decorative arts, and also those of book illustration. He asked Raoul Dufy to sketch his dresses; he employed the young Georges Lepape, and the caricaturist Paul Iribe; in 1908 he published *Les robes de Paul Poiret racontées par Paul Iribe,* a copy of which he sent to the wives of all the European sovereigns; the Queen of England, disturbed by such modernism, sent hers back. Two years later, he published *Les choses de Paul Poiret vues par Georges Lepape* (1911): 'Lepape came to see my creations, and drew them with wit. He cannot deny the part I have taken in his work, nor the influence I exercised on him; he was practically unknown . . ., his beautiful career has shown that I was in the right.' Poiret also published *Popolorepo, morceaux choisis par un imbécile et illustrés par un autre.*

With him the pre-war period came to an end, a period of affluence which had seen the origin of most of the movements which we still see developing today.

RAOUL DUFY. *La Chasse.* 1910. Woodcut

ANDRE DERAIN. *The Bridge at Cagnes.* C 1910. Etching

OSCAR KOKOSCHKA. *Hope Leads the Weak*. 1914. Lithograph

MAX BECKMANN. *The Declaration of War.* 1915. Etching

THE FIRST WORLD WAR

The 1914 War should have arrested the progress of modern art for several years—Villon, Segonzac, Goerg, Gromaire, Derain, Léger, Braque, Marcoussis, Laboureur, Paul Colin, Zadkine and many others were mobilized, and several were wounded. Boccioni died in the war; Jean-Paul Dubray came back half-paralyzed. Constant Permeke was wounded in 1914. August Macke died on the Champagne front in 1914, and Franz Marc at Verdun in 1916. Kahnweiler

84

had to cross into Switzerland. Yet that period saw the birth of the Dada movement in Zurich, with an exhibition including four prints and a drawing by Picasso done in 1916–17; this was one of the great periods of the Café Rotonde in Montparnasse; Jean Cocteau and Raymond Radiguet have depicted the gay life lead by soldiers on leave and war-shirkers; Madame Halika has described in her *Paris Moderne* how Paris 'had become used to a war which dragged on . . . the undercover dance-halls were in full swing . . . there were poetry and music matinées at Rosenberg's . . . all the cinemas were showing *Fairy Tales of New York* . . .'

Up to a certain point, the rear had accommodated itself to the war. The middle class and their children however, felt the war was a *nuisance,* and they bore the French soldiers a grudge. 'My brothers and sisters,' Raymond

ERNST BARLACH. *The Dog Snatcher*. 1915. Woodcut

ANDRÉ DUNOYER DE SEGONZAC. *The Dead Tree*. 1920. Drypoint

Radiguet recounted, 'were beginning to get annoyed with the war. They found it was lasting a long time. It deprived them of the sea-side. They were used to getting up late, but now they had to buy the newspapers at six o'clock.'

However, in *l'Elan* and *le Crapouillot* there appeared drawings sent from the front at Bois-le-Prêtre by a young artist, André Dunoyer de Segonzac. Their vigour and their superb graphic quality, so admirably adapted to the subject, were striking. Otherwise, the war inspired rather more ordinary works, which could be seen in numerous reviews and illustrated journals. Exceptions were the works of Guy Arnoux in the manner of folk art, and more especially those of Robert Bonfils (*Images symboliques de la Grande Guerre,* engraved on wood and hand-coloured in 1916), the *Mémorial des Alliés* by Bernard Naudin, and the Forains, even more famous for their captions than for the drawing: *Provided they can hold out—Who?—The civilians,* and the works of Abel Faivre in *l'Echo de Paris.* Only a few years later, in 1932, the lithographs of Luc-Albert Moreau recalled the trenches, the Bois des Caures, Douaumont and Verdun. As Segonzac said: 'Moreau has fought a heroic war. He has been very badly injured.' He remained obsessed with Verdun and we owe to this obsession the magnificent and poignant *Suite de Guerre,* which remained the only true evidence of the murderous war the infantry suffered. Still more heart-breaking is the evidence of Segonzac himself, in his series of drypoints illustrating Roland Dorgelès' novel *les Croix de bois* in 1921. Segonzac did not remain close to the text; like Dorgelès he wanted to show what he himself had seen and suffered. This series should be seen in its first state, where the drawing is very sensitive, for the publisher, René Blum, brother of Léon Blum, had the plates darkened, sauced as print makers say, for the final edition. These were the first published works by Segonzac, of whom more later. There was also a series of ten wood engravings by Marcel Gromaire in 1918, which are not as well-known as they deserve to be, entitled *l'Homme de troupe.* Another draughtsman and engraver, André Villeboeuf, who also fought in the infantry, did not make engravings of his memories, but wrote about them with the ironical title *C'était le bon. temps,* in 1933, through the eyes of a painter or draughtsman; the Verdun citadel 'from far off seemed a sea-urchin of earth, bristling with bayonets'; at the beginning of the war 'while enemy planes were dropping bombs in the

Les Tranchées dans le Village

JEAN-EMILE LABOUREUR. *The Trenches in the Village — VIII.* 1916. Line engraving

JEAN-LOUIS FORAIN. *Provided they hold out* . . . 1915. Lithograph

streets, the policeman went up on the roofs to empty their revolvers at those nasty birds'.

In Germany a rather poor album, the joint effort of many artists, the best being M. Oppenheimer (1885–1954), bearing the name *Krieg und Kunst,* appeared in 1916. The war prints of Oscar Graf (*Kriegsradierungen,* 1914–15 and 1915–16) were superior to these, as were the *Kriegslithographien* of Max Pechstein (1881–1955) published in 1917. We must also mention Otto Dix's striking allegories (*Die Krieg,* 1924) and E. Stern's plates on the 1918

ERNST BARLACH. *The Rocks*. 1921. Woodcut

Revolution. Oscar Kokoschka, who received a wound in the head, published in 1914 *The Bach Cantata,* a series of fourteen lithographs on the theme of war and of woman triumphing over man.

In England C. R. W. Nevison's magnificent prints of the war were among his best work. A noteworthy phenomenon was that artists were sent to the front as war painters, young artists especially, and this resulted for them in a recession from abstract art. Wyndham Lewis, who was an out and out abstract artist before 1914, has himself recounted how those miles of hideous

90

AUGUST JOHN. *Self-portrait with Hat.* 1919. Etching

desert they called the front line afforded him an austere subject-matter which made him give up his abstract style: abstract artists, who were the only ones he used to find interesting, now seemed to him cold and empty. The opposite reaction was Vallotton's. This expressionist, who, it is true, had not been called up, dreamed of abstract painting. He wanted to represent Apollo and Cleopatra not as characters, but as linear designs.

In the United States, the war did not inspire any remarkable works. The English, French and Germans, who suffered the most, were almost the only ones who conveyed its horror and its tragedy. The different governments, for reasons of propaganda, encouraged engraving, which they had ignored until then, but it was not the numerous official works which were to endure, but a few works of masters, of seers.

Part Two

THE POST-WAR PERIOD

The First World War caused no break in continuity, at least for the more commercial type of print. But we have already noted the appearance of Segonzac and Dix with their dramatic vision of the war; the Cubist movement, after being derided, became a subject of scandal, then of curiosity. Then came the Expressionist work of Grosz, with its enormous repercussions which are only now being appreciated. Expressionism, and Surrealism too, set themselves in opposition to the accepted classical tradition. Then followed the world slump and the withdrawal of artists within themselves, their obsession with the next war which they felt was approaching.

LABOUREUR AND ELEGANT CUBISM

The war and the post-war period saw the exploitation of Cubism, its adaptation to illustration, printed fabrics, wall-paper, posters and decoration, which had its hey-day at the Universal Exhibition of 1925. As early as 1919, Maurice Sachs noted that the word *Cubism* was all the rage among the Parisian public, and carried an aura of scandal: 'If people suspect a young man of unspeakable depravities, they say: he is a Cubist. For an adulterous woman in a good bourgeois family, *Cubism* again is the cause of it all.'

Jean-Emile Laboureur was a Cubist around 1913, but he only produced plates in the Cubist manner in 1916, the *Petites images de la guerre sur le front britannique*. These witty engravings also have a historical value, for they encouraged the group brought together by Vogel for the *Gazette du bon ton* to go into Cubism. Since 1913, each issue of this journal had contained coloured engravings and fashion prints, but these rose above the usual works of this type, by their artistic quality and by the worth of the artists who had contributed to them. After the war, Paul Poiret still ordered materials from Dufy, and from the photographer Man Ray.

MALCOLM OSBORNE. *Portrait of My Mother. C* 1916. Drypoint

GEORGE GROSZ. *Café at Night*. 1916. Etching

GEORGE GROSZ

George Grosz (1893–1959), worked as a caricaturist before the war, as early as 1910. During the war, in which he served in the infantry, he was sentenced to death for insubordination. He did most of his work between 1919 and 1929. He went to live in the United States in 1933, but long before that he was posing as an American in Berlin. He changed the spelling of his first name from Georg to George, adopted the dress and the manners of an American, and spoke German with what he conceived to be an American accent. The public was shocked by his drawings when they began to appear in the magazines: *Pleite* (Bankruptcy, 1919–24); *Jederman sein eigener Fussball* (every man his own football), and *Du blutige Ernst* (1919); *Gott mit uns* (1929: Grosz fined 5,000 marks for insulting the army); *Ecce Homo* (1923: Grosz fined

GEORGE GROSZ. *Parasites*. 1918. Pen drawing

EMILE NOLDE. *Dancer*. 1913. Lithograph

6,000 marks for outraging public morals); and *Untergrund* (1928: Grosz fined 2,000 marks for blasphemy). He was the only caricaturist of his time to be sentenced with such severity, but this was understandable—though not justifiable—because of the violent expression of his social satires, against war and above all against hypocrisy. Grosz's style is very original, with intentionally muddled sketches in which the various elements of his subject-matter are mingled like superimposed photographs. His figures are generally

97

drawn in profile, in order to stress their absurd or horrifying character: profiteers, prostitutes, criminals and down-and-outs are handled both with incision and with a fantasy prophetic of Chagall's *My Life*. The boldness and power of Grosz, who denounced Hitler in his drawings in 1923, placed him in the first rank. 'With Grosz, modern Germany has found her great historian,' Hanz Hess said. His influence outside Germany between 1922 and 1925 has not been sufficiently recognized. Grosz created types—the profiteer, the prostitute—as did his contemporaries Berthold Brecht and Kurt Weil. Henry Miller, describing a young woman in *Tropic of Capricorn*, refers to Grosz: 'Agnes was wringing her hands and praying out loud; she looked like a George Grosz idiot, one of those lopsided bitches with a rosary around the neck and yellow jaundice to boot.' This was not merely a casual reference; Grosz was a pervasive influence on Miller, as can be seen in *Tropic of Cancer*, first published in Paris in 1934.

On the occasion of a recent exhibition, Denys Sutton expressed his admiration for the incisiveness and eloquence of Grosz's line, and showed how his plates, with their terrible pessimism, express his pity for the tragic post-war period, in which profiteers were so successful because organized civilization had collapsed. Edouard Roditi has remarked that Grosz will always appear a minor artist, because he did not understand that 'his objections to the German social order could just as well have been made against the human condition', and because 'he had no political ideal'. Which is not to deny that his romantic view of thieves and prostitutes strikes a unique note, but Roditi preferred the German caricaturist Karl Arnold, who shows the same scenes but with less disgust and more fantasy.

GOERG AND GROMAIRE

The Edouard Goerg of the first period, of 1921, can be placed alongside Grosz. He was born in 1893, and after being held back for some years by the war, he began etching—and painting—in 1921. In reaction against his middle-class background, he did expressionist etchings, memorable for their cruel irony. For example *les Ennuyeux, la Demoiselle élue, le Bureau*

ANDRÉ LHOTE. *Wind on the Quarter*. 1925. Woodcut

LYONEL FEININGER. *The Trade Winds*. 1935. Lithograph

de placement, and the illustrations for *Ouvert la nuit* by Paul Morand, in 1922. We shall meet this artist several times, and will have new opportunities for admiring his talent and his steadfastness, for he put into practice his belief that print making should be done by the artist, and the artist alone.

Marcel Gromaire found his style in 1922, at the age of thirty, after fighting in the war up to 1919.

'Painting,' he said, and he could also have said etching, for he was an etcher of some importance, 'is for me a way of living, of perceiving life.' And he added: 'I am seeking to give man his place in nature.' His works are highly conscious and personal; they have always been noted for their dense, monumental quality, in reaction against the easiness and deliquescence of certain Expressionist works, and also against Cubism. They have been wrongly

100

compared with those of Goerg, with which they have no affinity. Gromaire believed in prints by professional print makers. 'The craft of the print maker is fascinating', he said, 'but only if the prints are original, that is entirely from the artist's own hand.' Gromaire put considerable work into his copper plates, pulling fourteen states of one particular etching, but without letting

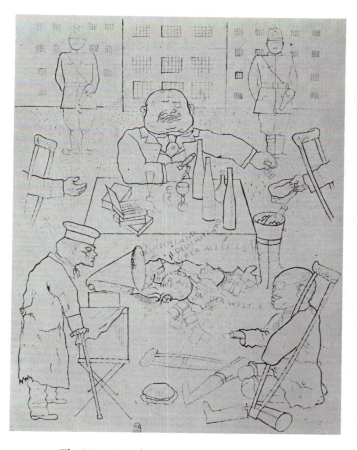

GEORGE GROSZ. *The War Cripples are Truly a Calamity!* 1920. Pen drawing

GEORGE GROSZ. *The Procurer*. 1919. Pen and wash drawing

MARCEL GROMAIRE. *Nude with a Vase of Flowers*. 1932. Etching

EDOUARD GOERG. *The Local Train*. 1930. Etching

it be noticeable. 'His style,' as Georges Boudaille said, 'grew more refined and simpler with the years, his palette grew lighter, and after 1928 his nudes began to appear.'

Gromaire, with a violence born of isolation, has frequently defended his aesthetic views. Form, he says, is the great mystery. 'To speak of formlessness is to speak of a music reduced to noises,' or again, 'the painting of the void, so much in fashion these days, has invoked a terrifying barrage of words to justify it.'

104

EDOUARD GOERG. *The Pretty Young Man*. 1928. Etching

Men from the North of France such as Gromaire, one of the few French artists born in the Sambre region, have preoccupations similar to those of Belgian artists and German Expressionists, such as Masereel, Barlach, Kirchner, Silovsky and Käthe Kollwitz.

Frans Masereel, born in Belgium in 1889 was one of the apostles of the social movement, and its most remarkable engraver. He lived in Paris from about 1910 and knew Romain Rolland, whose works he illustrated. The majority of his series of woodcuts were published in Geneva and Munich. He started in 1915 by illustrating books: Tolstoy, Georges Duhamel, Henri Barbusse, Zola, Villon; then from 1917 he published albums of woodcuts without texts, in a broad style, whose dark and tragic side is further emphasized by his handling of the wood, which is done in the manner of Vallotton, but without any element of anecdote or affectation. The titles of his series are revealing in themselves and do not call for further explanation: *Les morts parlent, Debout les morts, Vingt-cinq images de la passion d'un homme, la Ville, Figures et Grimaces, Juin '40, la Colère*. He has recently published a new album, *Poètes,* consisting of forty original woodcuts, and reissued his series *la Ville* (1925).

Avermaete has great admiration for him, both as an excellent craftsman and as an artist with an enormous capacity for work, the creator of a 'gigantic oeuvre'.

In Central Europe, Max Svabinski's teaching at the Prague Academy's School of Graphic Art was important. His pupils sought a simple, comprehensible and effective language. They ranged from pity for the unfortunate to celebrations of the sanctity of work and the voicing of social demands. V. Silovski (born in 1891), who lived in Paris from 1923 to 1926, depicted the prostitutes of the rue Montorgueil, the life of the workers, and the sufferings caused by misfortune. Jan Lambousek (born in 1895) illustrated life in the suburbs and in the cities and the harsh life of the workers. In 1922 he was in Paris; he depicted the boulevard de Clichy with the Moulin Rouge, at night, as an expression of sadness. About 1938, the Czech artists, and in particular K. Sokof (born in 1902) and K. Stech waged 'war against injustice' in much more violent tones. They were very much influenced by Rouault, Masereel

FRANS MASEREEL. Two woodcuts from *La Ville*. 1928.

and Steinlen; in 1928, Sokol called one of his lithographs *Revolution*. Stika
contrasted the figures in a cinema poster with two penurious lovers looking
at them.

Ernst Barlach (1870–1938) is now well-known and greatly admired; new
books on him continue to appear, his works are exhibited throughout the
world, his reflections on art have been collected in three volumes, and part
of his thousand-letter correspondence has been published by F. Dross.
This is indeed a reversal of fortune, for Barlach was the artist Hitler most
hated and persecuted. Hitler had his works seized, even from private
collections, he cancelled his commissions, had his sculptures destroyed, his
house demolished, and the artist died of grief in 1938 at the age of sixty-eight.
What Hitler hated in him was precisely what made Barlach's strength: his
successful representation of human life with its sadness and tragedy. Barlach

knew this life well, for like Munch he was the son of a doctor. After studying in Hamburg and Dresden, he spent the years 1895 to 1897 in France, where he did woodcuts of street scenes, influenced by Art Nouveau and by the memory of Van Gogh. In 1906 he had travelled in south Russia and had been

KÄTHE KOLLWITZ. *Self-portrait*. 1923. Woodcut

OTTO MÜLLER. *Two Nudes*. Lithograph

struck by the massive appearance of the peasants. From 1910 he lived as a hermit and mystic in Guestrou, in northern Germany. His best engravings seem to be those done between 1920 and 1925 (his engraved work comprises 300 pieces). They are the woodcuts of a sculptor, very black and very contrasted, and show peasants, beggars or tragic scenes from the *Walpurgisnacht*.

This romanticism of Barlach's is a long way from the art of Käthe Kollwitz (1867–1945), who also sought to express pity for the outcasts of fortune, but

KÄTHE KOLLWITZ. *The Widow*. 1922–3. Woodcut

with a kind of feminine tenderness. It is worth mentioning that her husband was a doctor among the poor in Berlin about 1891. Especially after 1928 she set out to portray destitution and the sufferings of the poor, in her expressively drawn etchings and lithographs. She enjoys considerable renown in Germany, Britain and the United States.

110

KÄTHE KOLLWITZ. *Portrait of a Man*. 1923. Woodcut

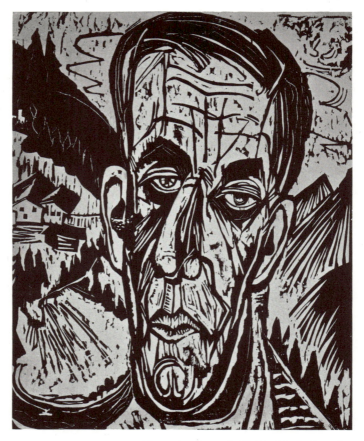

ERNST-LUDWIG KIRCHNER. *Portrait of van de Velde*. 1917. Woodcut

In a rather different style, Frank Brangwyn (1867–1956) showed the beauty of human effort and energy. We are no doubt unfair today to this good etcher, who was very much admired in his time, and had the exceptional honour of an exhibition at the Royal Academy, the first time a one-man show there was given to a living artist.

112

ERNST-LUDWIG KIRCHNER. *Portrait of Ludwig Schames.* 1917. Woodcut

MAX PECHSTEIN. *Two Heads*. 1919. Woodcut

It was in the early years of the post-war period that German Expressionism, born, as we have seen, in graphic art about 1906, attained its most powerful manifestation. The master was Ernst Ludwig Kirchner (born 1880, committed suicide in 1938). Kirchner engraved about 2,000 works, the first at the beginning of the century, mostly, like those of the other Expressionists, wood-

HEINRICH CAMPENDONK. *Nude*. 1920. Woodcut

cuts. Kirchner, a very great artist, is still virtually unknown outside Germany. His woodcuts from his paintings, portraits as well as landscapes, are extraordinarily original. He sought modernism neither in archaism, like Gauguin, nor through exact imitation of reality, like Lepère. He even did contrasted colour engravings, also from his paintings, which must certainly have

KARL SCHMIDT-ROTTLUFF. *The Kiss*. 1918. Woodcut

surprised the public between 1915 and 1930. His lithographs are also beautiful, but the woodcut seems to have been better suited to his inspiration.

Kirchner, as we have already mentioned, founded in 1905 the movement called the Brücke. His companions of that time, Schmidt-Rottluf and Pechstein were also artists of the post-war period. Karl Schmitt-Rottluf (born 1884), a friend of Kirchner, Nolde and Heckel, was persecuted by Hitler as a

116

'degenerate' artist. He is now a professor at the Berlin Academy of Fine Arts. He is a very personal artist, whose works are mostly bold woodcuts with large black areas, very strong in effect. Max Pechstein (1881–1955) who lived in Dresden and then in Berlin (and went to Paris in 1907) was also an excellent woodcutter and lithographer. It is tempting to set his lithographs of 1908–9 above his woodcuts of after 1918, which are less original. With these artists we must place Lionel Feininger (1871–1956), Otto Müller (born 1874) who did impressive portraits of adolescents, and Max Beckmann.

The Expressionism of these artists bears no relation to that of the engravers who preceded them, for unlike the latter, they did not use it to make social criticisms, but to achieve a more thorough study and a deeper understanding of the body, and especially of the human face.

Caricature cannot be separated from Expressionism; between 1933 and 1939 it was practised in France by Sennep and Jean Effel. Sennep (born in 1894) specialized in faces; the testimony he has left of the political world of the Third Republic is of great interest; his incredibly live portraits have created archetypal politicians: that of Edouard Herriot is a good example. He is a direct descendant of Daumier, the portrayor of Robert Macaire and Joseph Prudhomme. For him, the caption is merely ancillary. Not so for Jean Effel (born in 1908), by now like Sennep the creator of between 11,000 and 12,000 drawings. For Effel, who likes a good joke, captions count, and his admirers remember them and quote them. For example, in 1933, at the time of the American depression: 'Tissue paper is too dear, I'll wrap this up for you in a dollar bill.' In 1935 an associate says to Caillaux, the Minister of Finance, famous for his monocle: 'No, there's only a ten thousand million deficit. The last nought is your monocle which has fallen on the sum.' In 1937: 'What an idea to take grandpa to the Degas exhibition—now he's having his beard trimmed in the shape of a tutu'; in 1935, an Eskimo mother to her child: 'If you drink up your orange juice you can have a nice big glass of cod liver oil.' But Effel's drawing is also very witty, and all the more trenchant for its purity of line. Politically committed, Effel did his best drawings for the satirical weekly *Le Canard enchaîné* and for the Communist newspaper *L'Humanité*. We shall be mentioning these two artists again after 1944.

Pascin arrived in Paris from New York in 1921. An adviser to the Barnes Collection until his death in 1930, he played an even greater part as an illustrator than he did as an etcher, for his prints were little known at the time. Born in Bulgaria, the son of a grain merchant who was also engaged in banking, Julius Mordecai Pincas, known as Pascin, had already been to Paris in 1905 when he was twenty and he now remained there until the war in 1914. He had previously worked for *Simplicissimus* (1902), and done illustrations and etchings. He could be seen, dressed in a suit that was too tight for him, wearing a bowler hat that was too small for him, with a cigarette permanently in his mouth, at the *Dôme* with André Salmon. But his 1921 stay is of more importance. In 1925 he illustrated Pierre Mac-Orlan's *Aux Lumières de Paris* and *Fermé la nuit*, as well as *Trois petites filles de la rue* by André Warnod.

Pascin was one of the first artists of the Ecole de Paris to have come from central Europe. 'The Germans who reigned supreme at the *Dôme* and the *Rotonde* introduced ether and cocaine there about 1912.' When they returned after the war they came back to the 'affable and attractive Montparnasse, which is the centre of the world. More than ever, foreigners from all countries rubbed shoulders and conversed, often without understanding one another. The *Rotonde* and *Dôme* were to become their general headquarters.'

Pascin's eroticism was combined with a fine talent as an etcher. Together with Pascin we must mention Chas-Laborde (1886–1942), the illustrator of books by Carco and Mac-Orlan about 1921, whose great ambition was to become a painter, André Dignimont and Marcel Vertès. Dignimont, disgusted by the characters he saw drinking at the cafés, said of them: 'they are too ugly, they look too much like my drawings'. Vertès, who died recently at the age of sixty-eight, was born in Budapest. He worked in Paris and in the United States. In his albums as well as in his lithographs, he portrayed circus scenes with horses; he too had a certain feeling for eroticism, which comes out in his nervous drawing. Shortly before his death, he devoted a series of plates to the snobbery of the lovers of abstract art.

These artists all express the Paris of the post-war period, with its frenzied enjoyment, seen better by foreigners than by the French themselves. To learn

OTTO DIX. *Self-portrait. C* 1923. Woodcut

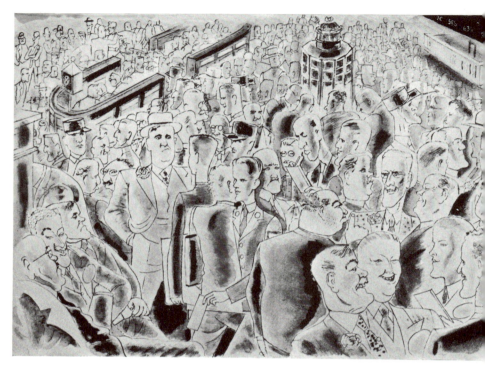

CHAS LABORDE. *Wall Street. C* 1930. Lithograph

about this epoch we must go to Maurice Sachs, a wonderful chronicler of those days: 'Paris was then living its victory. And with what ebullience! The boulevards jammed with cars bearing numberplates of every nation, and swarming with an exotic and motley crowd; the shop windows full, the restaurants, museums, nightclubs and hotels bulging with tourists, the festivals, the shows, the luxury and the debauchery: everything spelled out that the European capital of the post-war period was a merry woman, submissive to her tyrants and to her pimps. There was champagne in the air. The world had a war to forget.'

120

JULES PASCIN. *The Broken Jug.* 1929. Etching

GEORGES LEPAPE. *The White Hind*. 1916.

122

JEAN-EMILE LABOUREUR. *The Entomologist*. 1932. Line engraving

MARCEL VERTES. Illustration to Zola's *Nana*, published for its members by the Folio Soc
1956. Drypoint

Another aspect of this very violent post-war period was expressed in engraving by the intellectual Surrealism of Max Ernst, the lyrical Surrealism of Chagall and the Abstraction of Kandinsky.

According to André Breton, art has no place in Surrealism, which is only a means of expression and not an end in itself. Similarly, Dali declared that the Surrealists could neither paint nor engrave; moreover he added that 'technical points were but a minor preoccupation, since we wanted solely to register the images arising from our voluntary or involuntary *paranoia*'.

Before Marcel Duchamp had had his exhibition of *nudes without nudes* at the Montaigne gallery in 1922, Max Ernst (born 1891 in Brühl) had revitalized book illustration with an equally radical gesture. He replaced the traditional recipe of a text with pictures, by a new form, the album; he entirely did away with the text and even with the captions below the plates. His pictures were collages made from wood engravings which had been used in the illustrated publications of 1880, and which underwent a fantastic and often erotic transformation.

André Breton and Paul Eluard have spoken of the importance of this type of work, which found a place in reviews such as *La Révolution surréaliste* (1924–29). The first book illustrated by Max Ernst, published in Cologne in 1919 was *Fiat modes,* then *Miss Fork, Mister Knife,* consisting of twenty photogravures. *Histoire naturelle* was published in Paris by Jeanne Bucher in 1926 and the famous *Femme 100 têtes,* by Carrefour publications in 1929. Max Ernst pointed a new direction, and his historical and artistic importance is vital.

In 1924, Marie Laurencin had great success; in Paris her charming works were being published by Le Garrec, by the reviews *Sans Pareil* and *Nouvel Essor;* the Government bought some of them for the print room of the Louvre; Boulestin published some in London and Flechstein in Dusseldorf (from 1920). Some have judged her work harshly as Surrealism for snobs.

Such snobs have been ridiculed in a novel by Michel de Saint-Pierre, *Ce monde ancien.* The hero is visiting the Michel Colombe gallery with a friend, who shouts in his ear: ' "Look at that, one of the key-pieces of the exhibition! Ah, to see Duchamp's *Bride* and die." . . . He did not die. He was

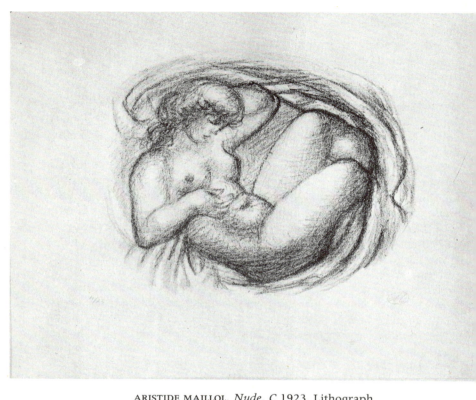

ARISTIDE MAILLOL. *Nude. C* 1923. Lithograph

wringing his hands, bending his head towards a red-painted nozzle and his eyes were misting. I have seen people go into raptures over a black triangle cut by a green square, entitled *Portrait of a woman*. I have seen strange attempts, nameless works which show a desperate desire to break loose from the ancient world and its dimensions. What a bric-à-brac: a weird mixture of histrionics, snobbism and sincere seeking.'

It was in 1930, at the high point of Surrealism, that Salvador Dali began to do book illustration, with a text by Louis Aragon and Paul Eluard, *L'Immaculée Conception*. Later, in 1935, inspired by the poet Lautréamont's *Chants de Maldoror*, he did forty-two etchings in a Surrealist manner. But it was his *Don Quixote*, a series of fifteen colour lithographs which revealed Dali's real talent as an illustrator.

CHAGALL

As early as 1922, Chagall's prints showed a hallucinated genius. Born in 1887, he started print making only at the age of thirty-five, on the advice of Hermann Struck. He began by illustrating his memoirs, *My life*, a book in which he considers the etchings as important as the text. He did them in Berlin, but he could not have the text published, for it was in Russian, and of his 110 etchings and drypoints he could only print twenty, which were published by Paul Cassirer in Berlin (1922–23). They express an obsession with death and the supernatural, a supernatural which seems normal to the artist; the figures move in a strange, dreamlike atmosphere, admirably suited to childhood memories.

During the same period, in Berlin and then in Paris, Chagall was trying his hand at various methods (etching, wood engraving and lithography), still representing animal-musicians and figures flying above the roofs. He expressed great pleasure at working in France: 'Paris is my second Vitebsk, my second birth-place', he said.

In Paris he was noticed by Vollard, who once again showed insight. He was keen to commission some book illustrations from him, but did not know which book; he felt that Chagall must illustrate a Russian text, but not knowing any, he suggested *le Général Dourakine* by the Comtesse de Ségur. But Chagall made his own choice, which was accepted: Gogol's *Dead Souls*, another satire on Russian society, perhaps not too far removed from Vollard's original choice. Chagall enthusiastically illustrated it with 107 full-page etchings. Like many of Vollard's books, it did not appear. It was only in 1943 that it was published by Tériade. This book was a great success; the numerous

127

SALVADOR DALI. *Illustration for Don Quixote*. 1957. Lithograph

figures in profile show astonishing types; the Expressionist influence is very noticeable and the Russian atmosphere admirably rendered.

In 1924, again for Vollard, who went on giving him work until 1939, he did *Acrobat with Violin* for an album of the *Peintres-Graveurs* which was not published, and the *Self-portrait with Grin*.

Chagall's art transcends all symbolism and all literary influences, and his contribution is immense. However, since his Russian-ness is an essential part of it, his influence over other engravers has been minor.

Without comparing him with Chagall, we must mention the fine prints of the same period (1924) by the Italian Carlo Carrá, born in 1881.

MARIE LAURENCIN. *Self-portrait*. 1927. Lithograph

MARC CHAGALL. *Self-portrait with Grin.* 1924. Lithograph

MARC CHAGALL. *Dead Souls*. 1923. Etching.

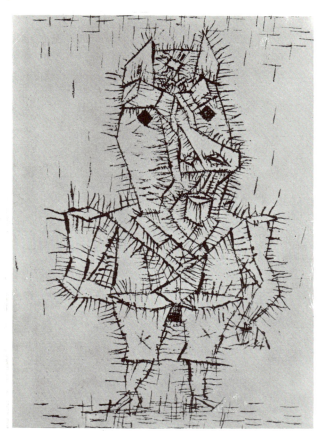

PAUL KLEE. *The Ass. C* 1921. Lithograph

ABSTRACT PRINTS IN 1922

Although he had painted his first abstract pictures about 1910 (he had discovered the possibilities of abstract work on seeing Monet's *Haystacks* in
1895), it was only in 1922 that Kandinsky did his first engravings, his *Kleine
Welten* (little worlds), published in Berlin by the Propylaen Verlag. At fifty-six,

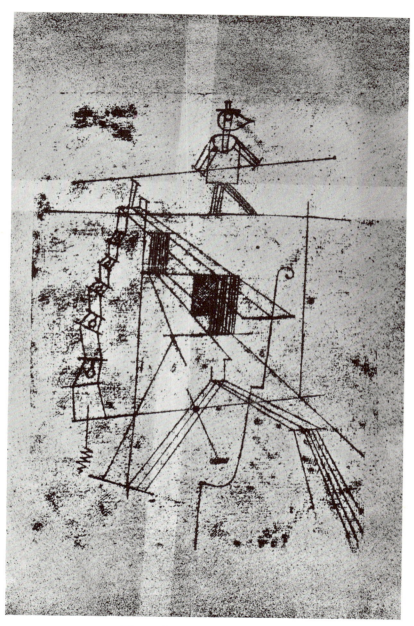

PAUL KLEE. *The Tight-rope Walker*. 1921. Lithograph

he already had a lifetime of experience behind him; he had worked in Berlin, Paris, Dresden and Munich. He had lived in Moscow during the First World War, after which he directed the Museum of Pictorial Culture and had been responsible for organizing twenty-two museums. He had taught Fine Arts at the University of Moscow, then returned to Berlin where he had his *Kleine Welten* published, taught between 1922 and 1923 at the Bauhaus, spent some years in travel and finally settled in Neuilly from 1933 until his death in 1944. The album comprised four colour lithographs, four wood engravings, and four copperplate engravings. This work, of which 230 copies were printed, is of great historical and aesthetic importance, although it originally went unnoticed, especially outside Germany.

Apart from Kandinsky's work there are few abstract prints from this period.

In concluding this study of the post-war period, we must note that, as historians of painting have pointed out, art had become international in a way it had not been before. Paris, and especially Montparnasse had become the meeting place of artists of all nations, where they lived or at least spent some time. Even Japanese prints, the most traditional of all, changed radically at this time, following the lead of the West. Yamamoto (1882–1946) was very much struck by a stay he made in Paris between 1912 and 1914, returning via Moscow. He started a school of print making in 1919, and declared that it was necessary to stop copying from the ancient books and to seek inspiration from nature. The following generation was even more influenced by the West; they professed 'horror' for the art of Harunobu which 'disgusted' them. They swore only by Munch and, later, Kandinsky, whose prints were reproduced in Tokyo, but saw no need to travel to Europe; this generation is represented by Koshiro Onchi (1891–1955) and Kiyoshi Saito, born in 1907.

FROM 1926 TO THE SLUMP

In examining this period we shall remain almost wholly in France, which is not to say that we shall only consider French-born artists, for the great masters, apart from Picasso, were Segonzac, Hayter and Chagall. But it was in France that they all did their best work. Paris was still the centre of graphic art, as of the other arts.

A few short years saw radical changes in graphic art, giving birth to a number of very disparate masterpieces, which were to lead artists for the next thirty years at least, in various, often opposing directions. The year 1926 is particularly important. It was the year of Byrd's flight over the North Pole, of the collapse of the franc, and of the proliferation of pictures, as Armand Lanoux said in one of his articles in the magazine *Arts*. This proliferation makes our task increasingly hard, and we are obliged to draw only provisional conclusions.

This was the beginning of an age of marked trends; on the one hand there were abstract artists, on the other, realists, all of roughly the same age. The abstract artists had the support of a very small group of intellectuals and of one or two reviews. On their side, the realists had public opinion, encouraged by the majority of the press. But there was also opposition from the professional engravers; pupils of the celebrated wood engraver Pannemaker or of the famous copperplate engravers, who were still alive in 1926.

Fortunately, a few galleries and a few dealers stood by the painter engravers in France. They deserve our admiration, for the movement was not so wide as the one which now flourishes around Saint Germain-des-Prés. The Sagot-Le-Garrec gallery backed the movement of the *Société des Peintres-Graveurs* and the Beaux-Arts gallery presented in 1937 an exhibition of 'young contemporary engraving' which excited considerable interest, with a lavish catalogue introduced by Raymond Cogniat. Henri Petiet, following Vollard's celebrated example, bought, and placed in his cellar, prints by Laboureur, Gromaire, Goerg, Boussingault and Segonzac, which he later published. Marcel Guiot commissioned two copper plates from Picasso, while Frapier, a dauntless publisher who disregarded public opinion, published small portfolios of prints by Bonnard and Matisse, which are now unobtainable.

Jeanne Bucher exhibited Hayter and Vieillard; and Mme Jacquard, Segonzac. Braque was known only on account of his book illustrations, especially his *Theogony of Hesiod,* to which we shall return, whose plates were to become collector's items.

In 1926, at the age of twenty-five, S. W. Hayter began his research into print making. He had noticed attempts at relief printing in nineteenth-century Japanese prints, and it had occurred to him, in order to emphasize relief in the print, to resort to elements of relief on the paper.

It must also be remembered that he had recently returned from a three-year stay in Persia, where he had imbibed the beauty of a non-figurative decorative art. Both these elements, the Japanese and the Persian, may account for the direction he was taking: Abstraction and relief. The public was guarded, his fellow etchers and wood engravers were indignant, but Hayter's *Atelier 17,* which he founded in Paris, attracted young artists, imposing new ideas on them and spreading a new outlook. We use the word 'imposing' because Hayter had a very strong personality and the works of his pupils are immediately recognizable, even though he may have tried to keep them away from too close an imitation. Hayter continued to engrave; in 1932 he showed at the Jeanne Bucher gallery an edition of the *Apocalypse,* the audacity of which caused a sensation.

One of the finest British engravers, John Buckland-Wright, when living in Paris in the years before the last war, worked with Hayter in *Atelier 17.* He went through a brief phase of abstracts in the Hayter manner but later remarked that for him Abstraction was like a tunnel: 'You have to go in, but God help you if you don't come out at the other end.'

A few years later, in 1935, Roger Vieillard (born in 1907), another of his more gifted pupils of the pre-war period, came to see Hayter. Vieillard had already done wire sculptures, like Cocteau, and now it seemed to him that 'line engraving could answer the problems of representing space with a very wide range of technical possibilities'. He became Hayter's pupil, but retained his originality. Bernard Dorival characterized him well: 'Great sureness of

MARC CHAGALL. *The Acrobats.* 1953. Lithograph

GEORGES BRAQUE. *The Theogony of Hesiod*. 1932. Etching.

STANLEY WILLIAM HAYTER. *Paysage anthropophage.* 1937. Etching

touch; a resolute line, incisive and sparing . . . on a desert of white seldom darkened by shadows.' And Dorival admired the 'powerful inventiveness' of Vieillard, though reproaching him with 'a hint of intellectualism'.

Another disciple of Hayter, whom Vieillard also knew, was Joseph Hecht (1891–1951), a Pole who had settled in Paris, who sought a sculptural effect in his line engravings, did his famous *Bisons* about 1929, and only came to relief engraving in 1949.

Shortly after Hayter, Hartung, whose beautiful style was inspired by explosions and flashes of lightning, made an important contribution to lithography with his shapes which knot together or pull apart from one another.

139

GEORGES BRAQUE. *Hélios mauve*. 1948. Lithograph

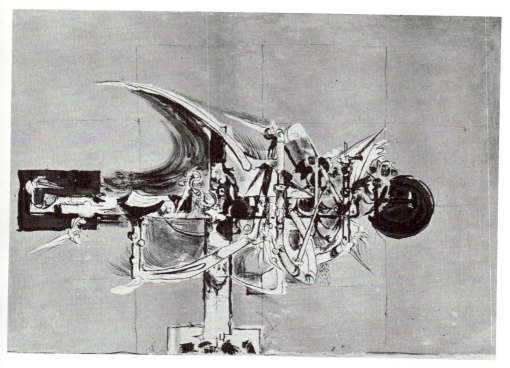

GRAHAM SUTHERLAND. *Crown of Thorns*. 1955. Lithograph

PICASSO AND DISTORTION

In 1926, Picasso turned to distortion. He had been tempted by Abstraction, to which he was drawn by his love of calligraphy; but he gave it up, and Braque who had discussed this with him, said that they had decided Abstraction would lead them to too incomplete a form of art: 'Abstract art did not acknowledge the fact that, by their presence alone, objects give rise to new states of consciousness in the artist.' But Picasso had fully realized that traditional representation of concrete shapes was impossible since the advent

141

MAX ERNST. *The Sap Rises*. 1929. Collage

of Cubism. They appeared dreadfully insipid, and it seemed very hard to see people as they were still being described in popular novels. In one of the most famous, Delly's *Magali* (about 1920, millions of copies sold, recommended for family reading and acclaimed by the Church), the heroine is described by the author (who was, in fact, two old maids) in the traditionally tender manner: 'This countenance, by the harmonious delicacy of its lines, by the proud grace of its expression, afforded the pure and admirable type of Grecian beauty which has brought fame to the women of Arles.' It was against these still too common aesthetics, and against those of the *Parisiennes*

101/200

MAX ERNST. *Two Silhouettes in a Marine Landscape.* C 1950. Colour lithograph

ETIENNE COURNAULT. *Grosse Tête*. 1929. Engraving and aquatint

painted by Jean-Gabriel Domergue, that Picasso wanted to react violently by showing his distorted faces with both eyes on the same side. Henceforward beauty was to be *convulsive*, Breton wrote in 1923; and Picasso denied that he had accomplished 'great deeds or made experiments'. It was just that, as he said to Sir Roland Penrose, 'each time I had something to say, I said it the way it had to be said, in accordance with what I felt'.

At this time, he returned to print making. While working on his sculptures at Boisgeloup, he also made the hundred plates which are known as the *Vollard Suite*. These etchings amount to a confession of the artist's anxiety when contemplating his work; Picasso offers us his works with 'anguished eyes', 'a furrow of perplexity on his brow', but also with the inventor's pride, for, as he himself said in 1923, 'to seek doesn't mean a thing; it's finding that is important'. He had always been preoccupied by his subject matter, and now he had become obsessed with it: is it the duty of the artist to depict the world and reality as the public expects them, i.e. in the form of a photographic imitation, or is he, on the other hand, to be free to treat this reality as he himself sees it, with the distortions imposed by his personal vision? This is the theme of the artist and his model: we see the model posing, the artist looking at the model, and then the round-headed, close-cropped artist tracing meanderings and scribbles on his canvas. Here again we find the love of calligraphy which characterizes Picasso, in his subject-matter as well as in his technique (he carried it so far as to work in pure line in 1934). His plates were now very light in key, with unhesitant lines and for the most part, no shading. From the series of copper plates, all of them so successful, Vollard selected 15 in 1932 to illustrate Balzac's *The Unknown Masterpiece*, whose text perfectly matches the brilliantly expressed anxiety of the etchings.

Their technique and sensitivity brought Picasso offers from publishers who wanted him to illustrate classical works, and in 1930 he did illustrations for Ovid's *Metamorphoses* published by Skira in 1931, *Hélène chez Archimède* published in 1931, and *Lysistrata* published in New York in 1934. Finally the etchings on the theme of *le Minotaure et le viol*, with their powerful atmosphere of erotic excitement, also form a confession, like all great works of art, and one can already see in them elements of *Guernica*.

Compared to Picasso, insufficient attention is given to Etienne Cournault, who created strange and masterly distortions in his etchings of 1929.

ANDRÉ DUNOYER DE SEGONZAC. *Bubu de Montparnasse*. 1928. Etching

Cournault was always interested in mirrors; as early as 1920, Doucet bought from him a great number of engraved mirrors. He was also the creator of *graffiti*, in the style of Klee and Kandinsky. We must bear in mind that the graffiti photographed on walls by Brassaï were photographed with the approval and on the advice of Picasso. At this point we must also mention the English artist John Piper (born 1903), who was in Paris in 1933, and who, like Picasso, was to do very successful work with the sugar aquatint process.

LUC-ALBERT MOREAU. *Physiologie de la boxe*. 1927. Lithograph

Illustrated books enjoyed considerable favour in this period. Illustrators were no longer specialists in the nineteenth-century manner, like Meissonier and his imitators. They were painters and print makers. They paid particular attention to harmonious layout, integrating the typography and the pictures. Daragnès was a master in this genre; his works comprise seventy illustrated volumes from 1919 on, the first *The Ballad of Reading Gaol*. But Daragnès' influence spread beyond his work, for he was a publisher, founder of the Edition de la Banderole; he was also a printer and an expert technical adviser.

The artists who illustrated books, quite rightly no longer wanted to stick closely to the text, as had been done in the past. André Jacquemin is interesting on this point: 'Although for me illustrating a book is a battle, I do not want to be a killer; I do not want to kill the dreams of the reader, all the images that his imagination conjurs up as he reads. I hate "literal" illustrations, illustrations which tend to reproduce exactly such and such a scene which the text evokes, of which each reader has his own vision.' He aims instead to echo the 'ideal contest' of the book.

It seems that the right conditions existed just then for the production of beautifully illustrated books: the presence of excellent technicians and a change in ideas about illustration. Unfortunately book societies, where experiment is easiest since there is no worry about financial viability, were still rather few and for the most part, timid. *Les Cent Bibliophiles, le Cercle parisien du livre, le Livre contemporain* and others were left behind by *les Exemplaires* who produced two beautiful books: *Adrienne Mesurat* illustrated by Alexeieff and *Amants, heureux amants* illustrated by Boussingault.

Publishers such as Briffaut and Babou who catered for lovers of slick eroticism employed Carlègle. Fayard and Ferenczi published cheap books illustrated with lino-cuts; a technique which probably came from Belgium where it triumphed in 1918 because of the high cost of wood in a ruined country. *Les Maîtres du livre* confined themselves to classical portraits as frontispieces (1911 to 1926 and especially about 1922). Fortunately *la Sirène* publications, under the influence of Fénéon, brought out in 1919 a Cendrars illustrated by Dufy, while the Nouvelle Revue Française published a Salmon illustrated by Derain, and a Gide illustrated by La Fresnaye.

ALEXANDER ALEXEIEFF. *The Name in the Wind*. 1928. Etching and aquatint

PABLO PICASSO. *The Minotaur*. 1933. Etching

Many of the finest illustrators were working at this time: Picasso, Segonzac, Chagall (*Les Péchés capitaux*, Kra, 1926), Hermine David (*le Grand Meaulnes*, Daragnès, 1930), Gromaire (*Baudelaire*, Quatre Chemins, 1926), Dufy (*Tartarin de Tarascon*, 100 lithographs). Kahnweiler published a Malraux illustrated by Léger and a Satie by Braque. Vollard brought out *la Sainte Monique* by Bonnard, Rouault's *Ubu,* and *la Belle Enfant* by Dufy; Skira, books illustrated

PABLO PICASSO. *The Sculptor's Studio*. 1933. Etching

PABLO PICASSO. *The Nude Model*. 1927. Copperplate etching

ANDRÉ DUNOYER DE SEGONZAC. *Colette at her Writing Desk. C* 1930. Etching

ANDRÉ DUNOYER DE SEGONZAC. *Corn Stacks in Ile-de-France. C* 1938. Etching

by Picasso, Matisse, Dali, and Beaudin; la Pléiade, two beautiful books by Alexandre Alexeieff: *The Brothers Karamazov* in 1929 and Gogol's *Diary of a Madman* in 1927.

Matisse often did illustrations; they do not follow the text; they are heads or dancing figures. As he explained to Charbonnier, 'Illustrations do not supply much; to illustrate a text does not mean to perfect a text.' 'Moreover,' he added, 'usually in my books the men of letters had not left me anything to do, they had said everything', hence his formula: 'One can decorate the

ANDRÉ DUNOYER DE SEGONZAC. *Pear Trees in the Midi. C* 1938. Etching

book with arabesques, keeping to the point of view of the writer.' This was also Braque's opinion.

It was slightly different with Picasso. When he illustrated his Buffon (1935), one of his best books, he was equally unconcerned with giving a literal interpretation to the text: his intention was to express his fondness of animals. Moreover, as Antonina Valentin said, at that time he felt 'the need to immerse himself in reality'. He worked fast, doing a plate a day, thus revealing, according to the same author, 'what an acute observer of reality he was, and

155

JEAN–EMILE LABOUREUR. *Autumn in the Marshes*. 1929. Etching

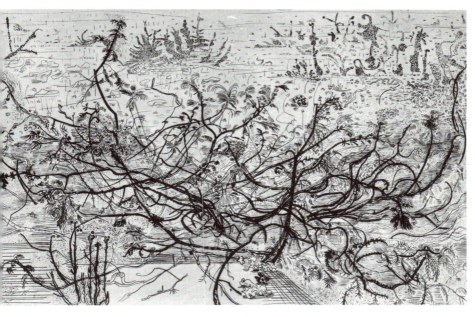

ANTHONY GROSS. *The Thicket*. 1932. Etching

at the same time, how far a complete change in style and technique can trigger off his inspiration'.

Vollard, after *Dead Souls,* continued from 1927 to 1930, to give work to Chagall, who illustrated La Fontaine's *Fables* for him. Vollard first wanted colour etchings in the style of the eighteenth century, and Chagall did about a hundred paintings in gouache which the engraver Potin declared impossible to execute; Chagall then decided to do them himself in black and white from different drawings, from which he produced strange and powerful works. When Vollard was reproached with having chosen a Slavonic artist to illustrate an essentially French book, the publisher answered that La Fontaine's inspiration was derived from the East, like that of Chagall.

Immediately after this, in 1931, and still for Vollard, Chagall did 105 etchings for the Bible, a book which had very personal resonances for him.

ERNST-LUDWIG KIRCHNER. *Mountain Landscape*. 1933. Woodcut

DUNOYER DE SEGONZAC

1926 was also a great period for Segonzac. He had begun print making much earlier, and we have already come across him before and during the First World War. After the war, from 1920, he returned to etching and developed it further. He had already done the *Morin* and the *Chaville* series. Now, in 1926, he reproduced the three masterpieces, *Le Modèle à genoux*, *Sport* and *Saint Tropez*. Segonzac is an authentic master of graphic art. Following Roger-Marx, Conil-Lacoste said not long ago that 'Segonzac's neo-realism is a little like an oasis, a rest period in contemporary art, the background of good workmanship and simple inspiration against which its most audacious

158

MAURICE UTRILLO. *Cabaret du Lapin Agile.* C 1930. Lithograph

PIERRE GUASTALLA. *Trees at Dieulefit*. C 1945. Etching

JEAN FRÉLAUT. *The Ile aux Moines*. 1934. Etching

elements stand out.' But this author was wrong in not having recognized that there are also extremely audacious elements in Segonzac. There is nothing academic about his drawing, even though the beauty of his delicate technique gives his work a classical character. Moreover such a 'rest period' was absolutely necessary and corresponded to the world's last few happy years. Segonzac poked fun, with his customary delicacy, at those who are bent on being thought geniuses who have made discoveries: 'The number of people

161

JACQUES BEURDELEY. *The Footbridge to the Wash-house*. 1927. Etching

who flatter themselves that they have invented or discovered something in art is just about the same as the number of fools. A strange coincidence.' On the other hand, he was well aware of the research of abstract artists, but 'regretted' that 'humanity and a feeling for nature, both elements of prime importance, were lacking in the works of Kandinsky and Braque'. He told Charbonnier why he etched as he did: 'I believe that art is simpler than these subtleties. I have left off my make-up, I have tried simply to remain sincere in the face of the marvellous spectacle of nature and of life', and again: 'When painting, drawing or etching in the country I enjoy communing with nature.'

162

He would do etchings directly from nature, taking his copper plates with him to the woods near Paris or in Provence. His plates, which appeared in series, and sometimes in volumes like the *Georgics,* are unforgettable. But he was not only the most marvellous of landscape etchers: he deserves admiration too for his portraits of Colette, Gide and Henri Mondor; Segonzac was fond of telling how long it took Gide to get used to his portrait, and how Colette accepted hers because her maid Pauline assured her that it really did look like her. Segonzac was also the best artist between the wars for depicting sport and athletes. In his illustrations for the novel *Bubu de Montparnesse* and *l'Appel du clown,* he finds a pretext for portraying faces and evoking atmospheres; *Thérèse Dorny dans sa loge* (1930) is one of his great successes.

LOUIS-JOSEPH SOULAS. *Landscape in Beauce.* 1941. Etching

Segonzac's enormous talent dominates a whole school rather than a mere group.

Among the masters of this school of landscape artists, which will surely go down to posterity as one of the finest expressions of French graphic art between the wars, Louis-Joseph Soulas (1905–54) delighted the public with his *Haystacks in Beauce* and was responsible for the renewed popularity of prints after 1928. André Jacquemin (born 1904) was already showing a

HERBERT LESPINASSE. *The Mysterious Voyages III*. 1938. Etching

EDOUARD GOERG. *The Birds Driven from The Sky*. 1938. Etching

marked personality in his work in 1926 and proved to have a very fine feeling for landscape etching. His heart remained in his native Lorraine, where from 1922 on he portrayed Epinal, Vaudemont and the surrounding countryside: he has been rightly acclaimed for his illustrations of Barrès' *la Colline inspirée*, which depicts this region. Nevertheless, it must not be forgotten that Jacquemin also did some good prints of the Brie region from 1933 to 1934, that he loved Provence and the Somme estuary, and that he illustrated Jean Giono's *Colline* in 1946 and Henri Bosco's *Le Mas Théotime* in 1948. Jacquemin, like Ciry and many others, was fond of expressing his admiration for Jean Frélaut (1879–1954), a painter engraver of Breton origin, who devoted the

JACQUES VILLON. *Chevreuse*. 1935. Etching

major part of his works, of which there are more than a thousand, to the
Morbihan region of Britanny. His etchings, which he began in 1903, were soon
to win fame for him, and he became particularly prolific after the First World
War, when his work was published by Maurice Le Garrec.

Pierre Dubreuil, who was born in 1891 and began working in 1911, is
best known for his landscapes of Britanny done between 1921 and 1930.

America too had a period of landscape engravers, the most famous being
John Taylor Arms (1887–1953). But he was very different from the French,
for while they remained close to painting, Arms was an architect. He founded
a school, encouraged young artists, wrote a treatise on engraving in 1934,
gave lectures and organized exhibitions. His best-known plate is a view of
Vézelay.

166

This school of landscape artists was able to have its work seen and appreciated by the public, thanks to the exhibitions of two print societies, the *Peintres-Graveurs français,* directed by Jacques Beltrand, and the *Jeune Gravure Contemporaine,* directed by Pierre Guastalla. Both talented print makers, these two men showed exemplary devotion to their colleagues and organized frequent exhibitions for them. *La Jeune Gravure,* founded in 1928 by eleven painters and made up of an invited membership including both expressionist and abstract artists.

The line engravings of Decaris (born 1901) can also be seen as part of this realist movement. Winner of the Prix de Rome in 1919 and a fine classical craftsman, he dashed off huge allegories and portraits with astonishing

MARCEL GROMAIRE. *The Sun in the Pines.* 1947. Etching

HENRY DE WAROQUIER. *Man's Face Turned Upwards*. 1934. Drypoint

HENRY DE WAROQUIER. *Head of a Man.* 1939. Colour woodcut

virtuosity. An engraving he exhibited in 1937 had war as its theme, and in 1940 he was the only artist to represent the French defeat.

Among these landscape engravers, two must be considered separately from the rest: Herbert Lespinasse and Anthony Gross. Lespinasse, a seaman, did seascapes which he made simultaneously real and imaginary, with altered proportions and enormous growths of seaweed. His woodcuts, done with unfashionable delicacy, have an intense poetry. Similarly, it is the poetic quality that is outstanding in the works of Anthony Gross, who etched forsaken gardens, brambles and thickets in the manner of Rodolphe Bresdin.

169

THE SLUMP, AND THE DECLARATION OF WAR

Print making seemed to have taken a propitious course, and could have been expected to win the public over, though perhaps in an appealing commercial form. But then came the slump; from 1929 it became extremely difficult for artists to find buyers for their work. Governments and municipalities, as well as private individuals, saw their budgets dwindling, while the number of unemployed rose by millions. The artists, abandoned by the public as they had been in 1850 with the advent of photography, were forced to work for themselves alone. This was the time when they stood most in need of friends and backers. Print makers found an illustrious ally in Paul Valéry, who in *les Nouvelles Littéraires* of 6 January 1934, published his famous *Discours aux Peintres-Graveurs*. In it he spoke eloquently of the joy of creative work and of the print maker's 'strange pleasure, a complex pleasure, a pleasure crossed with torment, mingled with sorrows, a pleasure whose pursuit lacks neither obstacles, nor bitter feelings, nor doubts, nor even despair'.

Once free of the public, print makers began to do increasingly experimental work. Villon, for example, returned to etching, and relinquishing his Cubism of 1911, sought a new figuration influenced by Abstraction, yet never quite taking leave of reality. Many of his key works are prints: landscapes, portraits and still life.

There were also a few seers who predicted the war: in the first rank was Henry de Waroquier, obsessed by the approach of death, pervaded by a feeling of anguish, of suffering and of impending tragedy. He was in marked contrast with his contemporaries, who dreamed only of pleasure and were strangely carefree. He expressed an 'imperious need to study the man who does not yet know he is to suffer, this call, this secret irresistible order, which compels me to search for marks of suffering on a face as the most human sign of beauty.' This is how we are to interpret his upturned faces with open mouths, terrified by the catastrophe which they feel impending.

Close to him, we find another seer, Goerg, the second Goerg we could say, the successor to the Expressionist of 1921. In a series of plates published by Petiet from 1934, he shows 'the forces unleashed', as he himself said. He warns us with *les Oiseaux chassés du ciel par les hommes,* he denounces *Lui Architecte,*

JEAN COCTEAU. *Poster for the Pushkin Exhibition.* 1937

i.e. Hitler (in 1939, this work was on the black list, among the prints to be banned during the German occupation), he represented *le Château sombre et ses environs, les Hommes et les Dieux* (published by Le Garrec, 1943). (C.f. in a different way, *les Visions intimes et rassurantes de la guerre* by Bruller, 1936.) These works and the beautiful view of Père-Lachaise cemetery (intended, together with the view of the illuminations on the Seine, for the Album *Paris '37*, which was never published), have a rare expressive and tragic quality.

France had a clear lead in print making during the period following the First World War. England and Germany had fewer important engravers. The United States were striving to form a school independent of Europe. This school found expression in an album entitled *A Treasury of American Prints*, which was published with a preface by Thomas Craven in 1939. This author showed that there was an incredible number of American print makers, that they were supported by State and municipal patronage, a

MICHEL CIRY. *The Fourteenth of July Banquet*. 1940. Etching and aquatint

HENRI MATISSE. *Woman Doing her Hair*. 1938. Linocut

system which existed nowhere else, that the Federal Government organized art 'like an industry', spending millions of dollars in subsidies. And he extolled the theme of the fortunate isolation of the Americans, and how wonderful it was to have at last a school free from French and English influence. 'Only the other day', he wrote, 'it seems our artists . . . were ashamed of the American label, and opposed with more vindictiveness than sense, to all efforts directed toward the formation of a native school.' Fortunately 'the succession of famous cults emanating from the studios of Paris is dead and, for the most part,

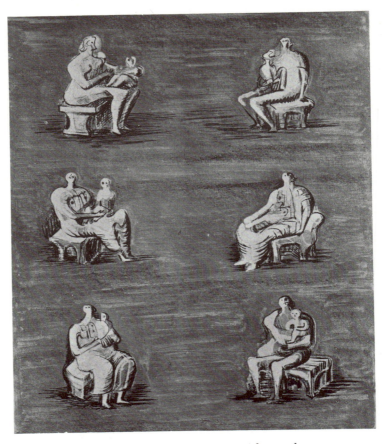

HENRY MOORE. *Composition*. Lithograph

forgotten; and the abortions of Surrealism—the culminating rot of European gadget makers—have found their proper level as eccentric window dressing for department stores.' Young artists were no longer turning towards Europe for their inspiration, 'our print makers are the best in the world', and Benton, one of the great American print makers of the time, remained true to the aesthetics of his homeland, even though he stayed in France during the heady years from 1909 to 1914.

These American print makers are certainly worthy of interest; their Expressionism has given us some fine pictures of American life and land-

WILLI BAUMEISTER. *Tennis Players*. Lithograph

scapes, by Buckfield, Cury, Reginald Marsch and Wood, but they are not works of the first rank. Their relative uniformity may be due to the fact that they were all printed by the same printer, a New Yorker called George Miller, considered by some a genius: according to Craven, the artist 'draws his picture on a stone slab with a grease pencil . . . and Miller does the rest'. Among these artists we must also mention Sloan, whose work for the newspapers gave excellent impressions of city life.

MARINO MARINI. *Horse. C* 1960. Colour etching

Part Three

FROM 1939 TO THE PRESENT

The Second World War caused a considerable generation gap, owing to the occupation of many countries, the internment of millions of people for up to six years, and the destruction and crime which affected virtually the whole of Europe.

In France there were few war artists. Decaris did engravings of the rout of June 1940, Soulas of the destruction and ruins of Orléans; Goerg, Yves Alix and J. Delpech showed Paris under the occupation; Galanis and especially Jacques Villon celebrated the Liberation. In Germany, C. Felix Muller and K. Rossing (both born in 1897) depicted the ruins of Berlin; Oscar Nerlingen evoked even more strikingly the destruction and the ruins of Dresden.

BEN NICHOLSON. *Still Life*. 1948. Drypoint

JACQUES VILLON. *Celestial Globe: the heavens*. 1944. Etching

And we must not forget the album published in Paris in 1944 by the Front National des Arts, which contains twelve lithographs by Pignon and Goerg; Mme Hervé, arrested with the manuscript of the preface by Paul Eluard, succeeded in swallowing it.

In England, the war inspired a very great artist, Henry Moore. Moore, who was in London in 1941, chose to do water-colour drawings rather than prints. There are, however, a few recent lithographs by him, of scenes from the underground, or of drawings for sculptures, which contain his outstanding qualities. He himself has said how exciting and strange he found the unbelievable scenes in the underground railway stations, which were used as air-raid shelters. Their platforms had an air of unreality, with the enormous number of people sleeping there and the uniform appearance given them by the blankets in which they were wrapped. A sculptor such as Moore must have felt tempted to portray them, and fortunately the importance and beauty of his works brought him an official commission for such scenes, thanks to the War Artists Advisory Committee.

It is worth giving a few details to help understand the art of Moore. Born in 1890, the son of a miner, he studied the simplified sculptures of Mexican and Negro art in the British Museum. He joined the army in 1917 and was gassed in France. He has explained that when sculpting, he did not proceed from modelling, but always from drawing.

THE NEW MARKET FOR PRINTS

An entirely different market for prints grew up after the Second World War. A different type of collector came into being. The collector who owned about a thousand carefully mounted prints, filed in specially made cabinets, men like Cognacq and Hachette, had disappeared and had been replaced by a large and varied public. The new rich looked down on prints, because they were not expensive enough and not immediate investments like paintings. On the other hand, prints were bought by interior decorators who hung them in the modern homes of their creation, and even had no qualms about glueing them on a wall or a door, thus unconsciously returning to a fifteenth-century

JEAN ATLAN. *Moonbird*. 1954. Colour lithograph

JACQUES VILLON. *The Conquest of the Air*. 1959. Colour lithograph

practice. They were also bought by young people to decorate their rooms; that is, those who were able to distinguish them from the multiplicity of colour reproductions on the market. They were sought by museums, especially in the United States, as well as by American and German universities.

In Poland the war brought about the rebirth of wood engraving, a paradox which has been explained by Julien Cain: 'During the dark hours of the German occupation, wood engravings were the testimony of the patriots.' These wood engravings were book plates: 'to assert one's right of ownership

WASSILY KANDINSKY. *Composition. C* 1940. Woodcut

was to stress the importance of books, the repositories of the native language of a country threatened with obliteration'.

These various factors led to a marked dispersal of works, as compared with the pre-war concentration; this dispersal will make the printed works of our time difficult to find in the future.

The method of selling prints was changing too. In place of the specialized dealers, who nevertheless retained a valuable stock, galleries and clubs of all kinds were selling prints. The dealers before 1939 had rarely published them; they had usually sold them for the artist on a commission basis, paying him annually after deducting their percentage. Now prints are often commissioned from artists by large international organizations who buy up entire runs of prints and sell them one by one, after exhibitions. Societies like the I.G.A.S. in New York, who bought several million plates over a few years, or like the Cailler Gallery in Paris, are increasing in number; they have their

GEOFFREY CLARKE. *Warrior III*. 1956. Sugar aquatint

ALFRED MANESSIER. *Composition*. 1944. Etching

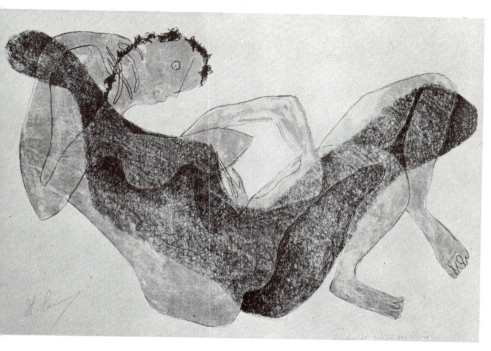

HENRI LAURENS. *Reclining Nude*. 1950. Lithograph

own subscribers, their regular clients. As they have large editions, they can offer a wide choice to the cultural organizations, without committing them-selves to any particular movement. The artists, like everybody else, can travel more easily and sell their own works in the course of their travels. As we have seen at different periods, their prints are necessary to make their paintings known. Miró explained to Charbonnier that he had not been able to achieve the contact with people which meant so much to him through easel painting, and that this was why he was doing lithography and wanted to print and sell millions of copies at very low prices.

The market was not glutted with prints, but was much more busy than

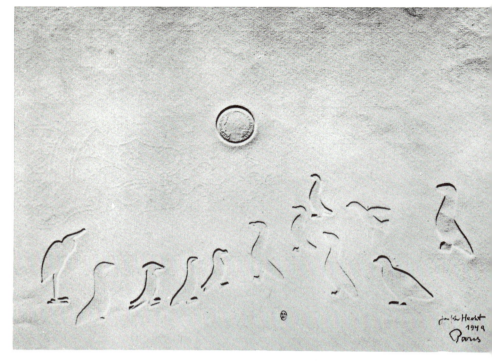

JOSEPH HECHT. *Penguins*. 1949. Relief etching

before the war. As at the time of the etching craze, everybody was doing prints: painters, young people at English, American and German universities, and members of the classes which were often set up in museums. These print makers, many of them casual ones who gave up prints and literature after university for business or teaching, did not seek their own expression. They would follow a teacher, work in a studio and confidently imitate their own master if he had a strong personality, or otherwise the great masters in fashion at the time. The masters were not all delighted with these imitations and tried to dissuade their imitators with loud protests. They were all the more anxious since, according to Picabia's witty remark, 'masterpieces do not have an influence; only second-rate works do'. Braque often spoke with irony of those who imitated the masters too closely; as Segonzac recalls for us, he said of certain young artists: 'They make wine-stains on the tablecloth, but all they can drink is water.'

JORIS MINNE. *The Weather Vane*. 1943. Etching

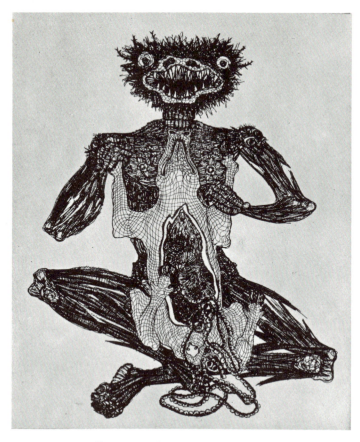

JACQUES HOUPLAIN. Illustration for *Les Chants de Maldoror*. 1947. Etching

ETCHING AND BOOK ILLUSTRATION

After the war, books illustrated by famous painters came back into fashion. During the war, publishers in the occupied countries, catering for the nouveaux riches who did not know how to spend their huge earnings, published many illustrated books, whose absence of quality has since become apparent. But in 1945, when Vollard's books were at last appearing, Skira and Tériade also published some fine books: Malraux's *les Conquérants* with etchings by André Masson, and other books illustrated by Picasso, Henri

LEONARD BASKIN. *Anatomical Man.* 1952. Woodcut

Laurens, Braque and Matisse with his wonderful graphic sense.

Similar books were also published in other countries, but they were little heard of. However, we know about those of Italian artists: original lithographs by Massimo Campigli in the *Lamento del Gabelliere* by R. Carrieri, published in 1957 by La Conchiglia in Milan; etchings by A. Chighine in *Un millione di anni* by the same author, published in 1963 by Scalabrini in Milan; lithograph illustrations by Carlo Leoni in *Poesia delle rose* by F. Fortini published in 1962 by Palmaverde in Bologna; twenty lithographs by F. Clerici in the *Bestiario* by L. Leonardi, published in 1941 by La Chimere in Milan. Similar books

189

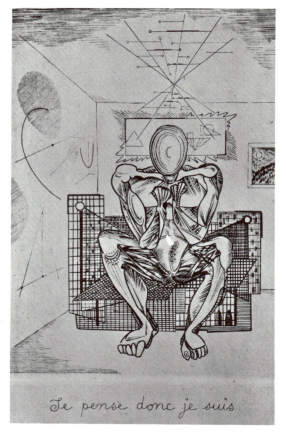

ROGER VIEILLARD. *Je pense donc je suis*. 1946. Etching

also existed in Switzerland, and in 1949 fifty-five La Fontaine Fables were published, illustrated by Otto Fischer.

If many of these books were illustrated with lithographs, others had etchings. There was even a renewal of etching, by artists ignorant of the technique. Prinner, in *Art d'aujourd'hui* has shown that certain effects happened by accident or even through ignorance, and that beginners sometimes obtained strange results: 'Once I had not noticed that there were a few drops of water on my zinc plate when I immersed it in the acid, and a few

ROGER VIEILLARD. *The Cathedral*. Drypoint

HENRI-GEORGES ADAM. *The Violin*. 1952. Etching

seconds later when I took it out again, it was swarming with rather artistic little beasts; each shape having its own light and shade—as if the nitric acid genie had been at work.' This idea led artists deliberately to exploit the accidental, and in 1949 this was actually the theme of a manifesto by Dubuffet. The learned Nordenfalk, in fact, said recently that this fortuitous art had an ancient origin, traces of which he found in a text written by Strindberg in France about 1894: *New Art Forms, or Chance in Artistic Creation.*

PICASSO, MOURLOT AND COLOUR LITHOGRAPHY

Did this mean the death of print making after 1945? Far from it. There were still many masters of the art, and fascinating experiments were taking place. Once more we meet Picasso, who through a remarkable piece of good fortune had returned to print making. Kahnweiler has told how in 1945, while most French people were shivering with cold in their homes, the great lithograph printer Mourlot had received a fuel allowance for his studio, so Picasso settled down in his home for the winter. 'It is the starting point of his admirable lithographic oeuvre which comprises hundreds of plates. He has revitalized the technique of lithography, and enriched it considerably.' And indeed, from November 1947, with wonderful fertility, Picasso drew on stone his heads of young women with long hair, his *Françoises*, his bullfights, his birds, *la Femme et le dormeur*, which is a key work, his fauns and his animals. Apparently he began his large series of paintings such as the *Meninas* and the *Déjeûners* with series of lithographs (1947) like the *David and Bathsheba*, after Cranach. We know that he worked from a reproduction of the painting in the Berlin museum; the compositions he did from this went through nine states and even then Mourlot said he would be very much surprised if the zinc plate did not go back to the artist for further working before being destroyed.

But Picasso left for Vallauris, and had to have Mourlot bring him lithographic ink and zinc plates; he used them very quickly, doing six pieces in a day. This is not an easy method, and so he decided to use linoleum, for he had discovered in Vallauris an intelligent and dedicated young printer,

ANDRÉ DUNOYER DE SEGONZAC. *André Gide Reading.* 1947. Etching

Arnéra, who could give him a proof as early as the next day. Kahnweiler has well expressed the 'monumental quality and the incredible vividness of the colours obtained by this completely new method'. Then Picasso had the young Jean Frélaut come and work with him on his etchings, particularly his bull-fights, which were published in Spain.

Picasso remains the most important figure in print making, but he was not the only one. Colour lithography was doing very well, and painters, delighted by their successes, used it a great deal. As early as 1945, Alfred Manessier admitted he had been 'surprised by the power of expression one could obtain with it'. Lithography used to be a medium without vigour; now it was beautifully rich in colour and contrasting textures. Manessier and Masson took it up; as did Robert Lotiron, though with a very different approach. So too did André Fougeron, whose forty plates of the French mining region are, as he says, 'a contribution to the formulation of a new French Realism';

MICHEL CIRY. *The Pity of Our Lady.* 1950. Etching

MICHEL CIRY. *Saint Sebastian*. 1950. Etching

and so did several of the artists who exibited at the *Peintres Témoins de leur Temps* from 1951.

In France, Goerg, Michel Ciry, Roger Chaplain-Midy, Pierre Clairin, Jean Carzou, Roland Oudot and Yves Brayer started doing colour lithography, and showed, like Maurice Brianchon, how they took to this 'thick line of chalk and ink'. One of the great artists of colour lithography is Chagall who as early as 1944, when he was still in New York, and then in 1948–50 in Paris, shows us the Eiffel Tower, Notre-Dame or lovers in the sky, with his usual poetic feeling.

Since the Second World War, prints in colour have enjoyed a great vogue. We must admit that this could mean that people are seeking a substitute for painting—for the painting of masters which they hear so much about—but something better than reproductions of paintings. Good judges were anxious, and Claude Roger-Marx wondered if someone might decide to colour in Rembrandt's *Hundred Guilder Plate*. But this movement towards colour was universal, and manifested itself in countless ways; films were in colour, and so were houses, all the fittings and even the linen. Should or can prints remain outside this fashion, this taste? Jean Le Moal said to Charbonnier that black and white prints were 'extremely intimate and perhaps too discreet' and that this was one of the reasons for their limited appeal. 'I believe,' he added, 'that our age needs colour.'

Lithographic printers were of the same opinion, particularly Mourlot. He had printed colour lithographs by Picasso and other great painters, and colour, which was also used by Hayter and the abstract artists, had spread over the world. This victory was acknowledged even in the United States where colour lithography had one apostle, G. von Oroschwitz, then curator of the Cincinnati Museum. With the help of the great collector Albert P. Prietman, he organized colour lithography Biennials from 1950. The first was not a success: of the 250 prints from fourteen countries, only nineteen were sold. But the second Biennial was sufficiently noticed for a selection of the best works to be sent to England, Germany and Switzerland. In 1956, at the fourth Biennial, thirty-two countries took part and the exhibition was inaugurated by the director of the New York Museum of Modern Art. It was mentioned in *Time* magazine and 300 prints were sold. In 1957 a Biennial of the same kind was inaugurated in Tokyo. Another proof of success was that

PABLO PICASSO. *Françoise in the Sun. 15 June 1946.* Lithograph

the English newspapers said that colour lithography was 'the only popular form of art in England, which in spite of its low prices, had all the good qualities of contemporary art.'

In connection with colour lithography in the United States, we must mention the remarkable endeavour of the Tamarind Workshop, set up in 1958 by Mrs J. Wayne, where both lithographers and printers learned their skills. This interesting venture had the backing of the Ford Foundation.

Does this popular art produce genuine, original prints, collectors and dealers ask themselves. A current enquiry by the Print Council will shed light on this point. Will the medium be vindicated or condemned? Probably both.

REBIRTH OF WOOD ENGRAVING

Apart from lithography and etching, the post-war period saw the rebirth of wood engraving, especially in Switzerland. In 1953, an international society of wood engravers was founded in Zurich, under the name of *Xylon*. This group looks back to fifteenth-century engraving, especially coloured wood engraving, for its members do not want just 'grim black and white'. In the introduction to the catalogue of their exhibition at Vienna in October 1961, they pointed out that wood engraving should draw its inspiration from the Gargas cave in the Pyrenees, 'where you can see imprints of mutilated hands done with a primitive paint made of iron oxide and animal fat'. In spite of their manifesto, several artists have hesitated between nineteenth-century traditionalism and the influence of Gauguin, but there are among them marked personalities like H. R. Bosshard (born in 1929 in Zurich), Werner Hoffmann (born in 1935 in Affoltern), and Heinz Keller (born in 1928 in Winterthur). Nearly all of them are Expressionists, for wood does not lend itself well to Abstract art, and moreover, they say their forbears of the fifteenth century had such power of expression that they were the ancestors of modern Expressionism.

FERNAND LÉGER. *Composition. C* 1950. Colour lithograph

CARICATURE AND CHILDREN'S DRAWINGS

We meet Expressionism again in drawings for newspapers, to which we must turn once more because of their importance in connection with original engraving; the great master of the post-war period is Saul Steinberg. Born in 1914 near Bucarest, he studied sociology then architecture, before working for the *New Yorker* from 1941, and establishing himself in New York in 1942. Albums of his drawings were also published: *All in Line,* 200 drawings (New York, 1945); *the Passport* (London, 1954).

One often speaks of the *genius* of this great artist, the master and symbol of modern American caricature, who has so wittily depicted the absurd life of modern man. Gaiety, as Naef says, is missing from his laughter, as it will often be in future from the art of caricature.

'With Steinberg,' wrote Jacques Sternberg in *Arts* in 1956, 'the cartoon very nearly made its entry into Parisian society a few years ago, and at the

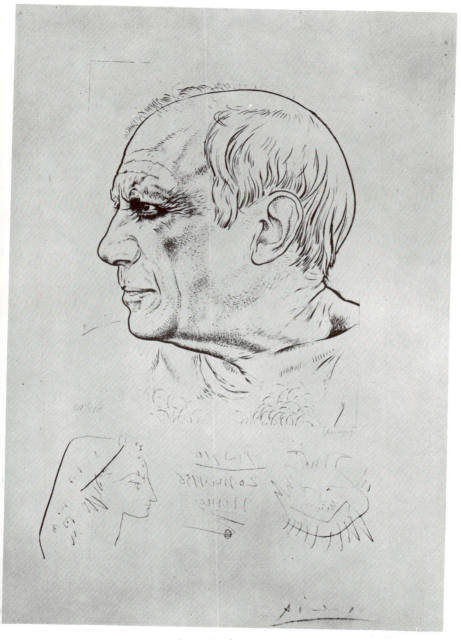

PAUL LEMAGNY. *Portrait of Picasso.* 1956. Etching

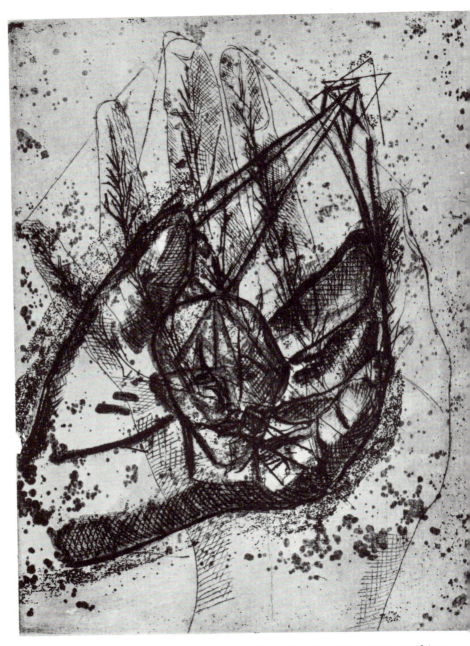

GERMAINE RICHIER. *In Honour of the Hand: the Head-Line*. 1949. Etching

same time into the domain of things to be grasped by the world's tentacles. By some miracle, it didn't happen: Steinberg was too good a draughtsman, his genius for commas and arabesques was too obvious; he was not taken for a caricaturist but for a draughtsman, which is as much as to say for an artist . . . And caricature remained a genre with no precise definition.'

In France, Dubout is still working, and his caricatures are very much appreciated. With their comical crowding up of grotesquely, hallucinatedly marked types, they even influence present-day literature. In the detective novels of Fréderic Dard (Commissaire San Antonio), we find 'the old man running a narrow, pale tongue over his absence of lips, . . . his face as patched as an old inner tube, his crushed nose, his ears in tatters, his eyes asquint.' Bérurier, who 'gets hold of a hair in his nose, yanks it out with a sharp pull, wipes away the tears resulting from this operation, and scrutinizes it attentively', is again straight out of Dubout.

With him, we must mention Chaval, Mosé, Henry, Tim and François, who had an album, *Manigances*, published by Delpire with a preface in which

SIEGFRIED KORTEMEIER. *Still Life*. 1950. Sugar aquatint

MICHEL CIRY. *Houseboat at Rueil*. 1950. Etching

Pierre Dumayet apologized for speaking of a caricaturist, Siné, whose first album came out in 1956 when he was twenty-eight, with 'horrible details and a preface by Marcel Aymé', and whose lack of respect for both 'his subjects and their treatment' has continued to increase. More interesting still is the psychotic world of the cartoons of Roland Topor.

In England there are Ronald Searle, the creator of a strangely sadistic world of monsters, and Gerald Scarfe whose caricature is particularly brilliant and vicious. In the United States, there are Charles Addams, with his black humour, who gives us images of terror and cruelty; Sogglow; Day, and Virgil Partch, *Collier's* 'gagman', who was ordered by the British high command to cease his attacks against the army. The *New Yorker* played a considerable part, animated by S. J. Perelman, also scriptwriter for the Marx Brothers' films. Sternberg, from whom we have borrowed some of the above facts, stresses the themes of modern American caricature, which are an obsession with money, the vagaries of big business, the monotony and absurdity of life on earth. Caricature is a difficult art; it requires constant searching for

ROBERT LOTIRON. *The Chestnut Trees. C* 1950. Lithograph

JOHN BUCKLAND-WRIGHT. *Three Bathers*. Wood engraving

FRANK MARTIN. *Mathilde de la Mole*. Illustration to Stendhal's *Le Rouge et le Noir*, published for its members by the Folio Society. 1965. Wood engraving

ideas, great inventiveness, a fertile imagination and permanent virulence. Sempé has explained that a humorist is not necessarily funny in everyday life, and has said how sorry he is that his 'strange calling' should not be taken seriously. As Werner Hofmann said, caricature has had a great influence on the art of today. Art also has become obsessed with not only the tragedy but also the absurdity of life; 'disproportion and grimace have taken hold of our existence' and we have become 'indifferent to the primordial tensions between the beautiful and the ugly'.

At the same time as for caricature, interest arose in children's drawings, especially between 1945 and 1950, though like the interest in folk art, it has been decreasing ever since. French avant-garde reviews such as *Art d'aujourd'hui* were passionately scrutinizing the drawings of children from four to eight years old, and saying things like, 'the little men are epic little men . . . This humanity is monstrous, but how expressive it is'

These two movements, as we have already said, had a great influence. They can be linked with Dubuffet's extraordinary portraits (*Plus beaux qu'ils ne croient,* after 1946), thus commented upon by the artist: 'funny noses, thick mouths, crooked teeth, hairs in the ears, I have nothing against all that . . . I believe that the most sketchy portrait, so long as it contains even a little of this element, will be of more use to me than the most studied one possible.'

STANLEY WILLIAM HAYTER. *Couple.* 1952. Etching and engraving

THE NEW PRINT MAKING

From now on, the centre of print making is once again Paris. This is universally conceded, in spite of national susceptibilities. The fact is even mentioned in an introduction by F. Schiff to the catalogue of the exhibition of European prints in Haifa in 1962.

ABSTRACTION AND THE ECOLE DE PARIS

But what is this new print making? Some assert that it is abstract, that it must be abstract and so dominate the world. As for the abstract prints, which are given generous wall-space in international exhibitions, they are of an absolute uniformity; one cannot distinguish a French print from one done in Africa, the United States or Chile. The Brazilian review *Modulo* notes the absence of local colour and of themes peculiar to Brazil; one can establish the same fact everywhere. This is a very serious matter. Wise men such as Bersier have put their finger on it: 'Personal experience,' he writes, 'is often sadly lacking in an art which is losing strength by repeating itself in the same arbitrary form. Without roots of its own, it cannot renew itself, for the sap cannot rise. Grafting and layering are increasingly taking the place of sowing. We have flowers,' he concludes, 'but we will not have corn.' This state of affairs is the fault of international art criticism, which has attempted to coerce public opinion; the latter is, however, beginning to react vigorously.

As Max Ernst said in 1959, although abstract art has a considerable place in the United States 'on the surface', for it is taught in museums and extolled in reviews, 'the more aware among the painters in this movement fully realize the danger of sterility which this ease of success represents for them'. In Ernst's words, 'Abstract art is the dried fruit of a correct argument.' And Matisse said of abstraction: 'It is just a method which artists have always used. But one must not be led into temptation, must not become a dupe of the method while trying it out.'

And many people understand that the essential problem of our times is to 'reconcile the abstract values of form and colour with the concept of space

ROLAND OUDOT. *Harvest.* C 1955. Lithograph

and the portrayal of the subject.' Denys Sutton who has said everything that
has to be said about the great masters of the abstract, now writes: 'Our elders
are still bound up with Abstraction and the exploration of sensibility; but
young artists are seeking more substantial matter. They seek a contemporary
theme which they usually take from urban life.'

Nobody denies the value of Abstraction, whose masters are Hayter and
Friedlaender as well as Atlan and Manessier. One ought to study the relation-

JOAN MIRÓ. *Sad Traveller*. 1955. Colour lithograph

ships between abstract art, prints and calligraphy. A painting by Klee, dated 1940 called *Ecriture* conveys certain of these relationships. Mark Tobey, giving one of his works the title *Calligraphy* also shows his wish to 'write his painting'. Jackson Pollock (1912–56) made no secret of his interest in Chinese calligraphy, an interest shared by de Kooning and the early Soulages.

One ought also to analyze the considerable influence of aerial photography on abstract art, and that of scientific photographs showing molecules, which made Henry Moore say, 'There is in nature a limitless variety of shapes and rhythms (and the telescope and microscope have enlarged the field) from which the sculptor can enlarge his form-knowledge experience.'

JEAN-JOACHIM-JACQUES RIGAL. *The Luxembourg Gardens. C* 1955. Etching

JOSEPH HECHT. *Leopards Hunting*. Line engraving

Hayter's *Atelier 17* had considerable importance after the war; Hayter published his famous book *New Ways of Gravure* in New York in 1946, and in the same year Sir Herbert Read devoted a book to him. Hayter's originality and talent explain his worldwide influence, but some consider that many of his pupils have shown too slavish an admiration for his prints. From 1940 to 1955, he had a studio in New York similar to the one he had had in Paris. Foremost among those who worked through Hayter's influence and found a highly personal style was John Buckland-Wright, a former pupil of *Atelier 17,* who became head of the etching and engraving classes at the Slade School in London in 1950.

214

JEAN CARZOU. *Roussillon.* 1962. Colour lithograph

Mauricio Lasansky, the director of the Iowa studio and Gaspard Peterdi, the director of the Brooklyn Museum are counted among Hayter's admirers. Friedlaender, who opened a studio in 1950 and who is an excellent teacher as well as a great artist, is in the same case as Hayter, but he is on his guard and, in a recent interview, said that he wanted his pupils to express themselves freely, even outside the forms he liked: 'I look among their efforts for things which seem to be leading in a fruitful direction. But while letting them open out in their own way, I try to prevent them from doing Friedlaenders.'

DOLF REISER. *Flight Forms*. Line engraving and soft ground etching

ANDRÉ MINAUX. *Still Life*. 1950. Lithograph

SURREALISM AND EROTICISM

Surrealism nowadays is not dead whatever one may say, and although Chirico has called it 'a bottled joke', it is still of interest, and may be one form of the new figuration. The most famous surrealist print maker is Lucien Coutaud (born 1904). Coutaud has often said he cannot conceive of art without eroticism. 'I cannot imagine,' he said to Charbonnier, 'a woman without buttocks'; he sees eroticism in the whole of nature, and asserts that 'nothing

217

LUCIEN COUTAUD. *Young Person from near Joucas*. 1949. Etching

OTTO FISCHER. *The Wonderful Monsters I*. 1950. Drypoint

looks more like a pair of buttocks than an apricot'. His art, which he himself
has dubbed 'erotomagic', has been fostered by his southern temperament,
his admiration for Sade and his acquaintance with the arcana of the print
rooms. But he adds to eroticism an extraordinary feeling for magic, which
puts him in a class of his own. His engraved work was begun in 1932, but he
abandoned it shortly thereafter and resumed it only after 1945. He has often
depicted a dream figure with a body separated in two, surrounded by spikes
and leaves; Coutaud has partly explained this by saying that these thorns
were a means of defense against a cruel world. Eroticism is always subversive,
as Masson who, like Georges Bataille, has made a study of it, has rightly
pointed out. Dali too has shown the truth of this in his etchings.

FERDINAND SPRINGER. *Eupalinos*. 1946. Etching

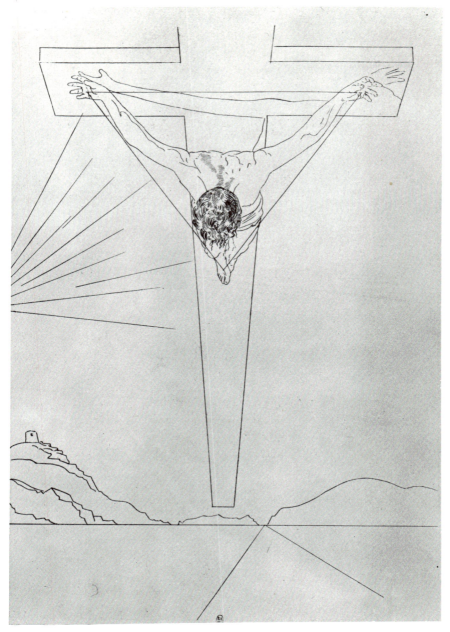

SALVADOR DALI. *Christ Crucified*. 1951. Etching

PIERRE-YVES TREMOIS. *The Faun*. 1947. Line engraving

OSCAR KOKOSCHKA. *The Magical Shape*. 1952. Lithograph

BERNARD BUFFET. *Toreador*. 1959. Etching

MISCH KOHN. *Bullfight*. Wood engraving

FIGURATIVE ART

But there are other approaches which undoubtedly have a future. Bernard Buffet, who represents one of them, has said, 'I believe that the abstract experiment is a blind alley, an invention of tired intellectuals.' Others, such as Segonzac, have said with irony that 'fidelity to nature has become a new kind of independence in art'. In 1960 Goerg wrote an open letter to André Malraux on the question of Abstraction.

Among these artists who did not give in is Buffet (born in 1928), one of the best contemporary engravers. He does not seek to please, but to express his pain and desolation in the face of a horrifying universe. His *Passion of Christ* (1954, 21 plates, 140 copies), his landscapes, deserted even when they are views of New York, have an undeniable power.

Michel Ciry (born 1919) had, as Bernard Champigneulle says, an art which consists of discretion and sacrifice. But he has gained in power; his religious plates, done in a fine Christian spirit, are etched with a firm and sober technique. One can but admire this sad religious artist, obsessed with the faces of the old, saintly nuns of Assisi.

Alberto Giacometti (born 1901) is a little older, but he is linked with this movement. 'I see something, I find it wonderful, I want to try to represent it,' he said around 1955. His drawings on transfer paper become excellent lithographs which, for some unknown reason, the official mouthpiece of his publisher *Derrière le miroir*, considers distinctly inferior to his etchings.

He tries to represent objects, but in a very different way from the ancients (whom he knows well, since he has long frequented the museums). He has subjected himself to the making of innumerable copies, but he had a justification in 1921, at least, for his profound sense of ceaseless transformation in life, when he saw the change after death in a friend's face. Excluded from the surrealist group in 1935, he was not at that time accepted by the realists, but through his prescience and his genius he is at the origin of present-day realism, so different from what it used to be. One rarely notes in his lithographic works—still little known and little exhibited—the obsession with sexual murder of which his commentators speak, and which caused him in April 1945 to write of his admiration for Callot's *Misères de la guerre*.

It is tempting to compare Giacometti with André Minaux, another solitary artist, creator of admirable, strongly constructed still life, who now, with his jagged hulls of boats, is initiating a movement towards an *other* reality.

Auguste Gaudin, who lives in Douai, in the north of France, and whose work is now rarely seen, belongs to the same generation. Between 1945 and 1950, after suffering badly as a prisoner, he showed a series of etchings and lithographs, tragic works, pictures of hanged men or landscapes under rain or storm, broken up by telegraph wires, which in the countryside take on the aspect of scarecrows, more alive than the old poles of long ago. Jansem, a younger artist, with great talent, expresses a poignant *misérabilisme*. Edouard Pignon and the etcher Ramondot also deserve mention.

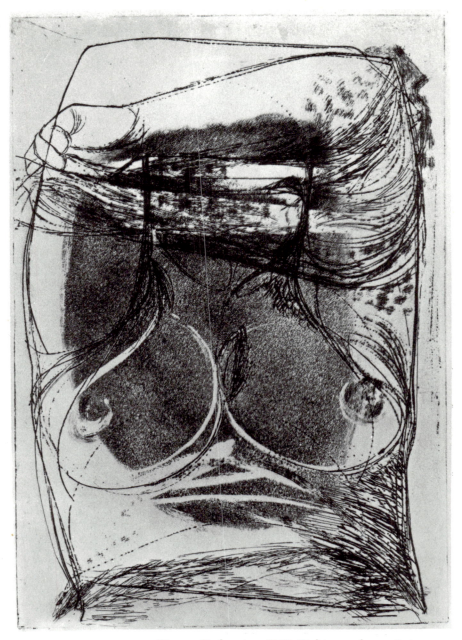

NIGEL LAMBOURNE. *Woman Undressing*. 1962. Etching and aquatint

What is beginning to be called the new figuration is seen in engraving as well as in painting. One of its representatives, Bernard Dufour, goes a very long way. For him, etching is *'the instrument of a language,* an instrument which at first I wanted to be poor, simple, impoverished so to speak. But the thinness of the line drawn by the point, the lack of charm of the furrow in the black ground down to the polished copper . . . made it apparent to me what the drawing was losing by being abstract . . . I needed . . . the scored copper plate itself to speak, to tell a story, whose power would already be obvious even in this lifeless drawing. Hence the arrival of the image on my plates.'

TEXTURE AND RELIEF PRINTING

Also after the war, the sculptor Henri-Georges Adam who had been doing somewhat expressionist engravings since 1934 showed his new line engravings on copper: *Mai ou la bête à cornes, Juin ou la femme pot, Dalles, sable et eau, Ombres gravées.* Jean Cassou, who had always given him his support, gave him a magnificent and well deserved eulogy in 1961: 'Born an engraver, it is from engraving that he set out to conquer the world. His engravings have become increasingly powerful, and the extraordinary grandeur of the workmanship expressed in them has been easily given free play in the field of sculpture.' The opinion of another great sculptor, Henry Moore, can be quoted with reference to Adam, who sculpted the pierced stone at the museum of Le Havre: 'The first hole made through a piece of stone is a revelation . . . A hole can itself have as much shape-meaning as a solid mass. Sculpture in air is possible, where the stone contains only the hole, which is the intended and considered form.'

In engraving, the texture now plays a great part. Like many other artists, Joan Miró affirms this: 'The feeling for texture is of prime importance. *Texture dictates everything;* I am against any intellectual refinement, which is preconceived and dead.'

The preoccupation of Courtin and Vieillard with questions of texture leads them to modify traditional engraving. According to Pierre Courtin (born in 1921), prints are 'objects intended to give tactile pleasure', prints

PABLO PICASSO. *The Woman at the Mirror*. 1950. Colour lithograph

need to be seen laid flat, free, uncovered, never stuck on a mount or covered with glass. He made relief line engravings. In a similar spirit, Vieillard writes: 'Etching, like painting, starts from the surface, from the colour, or at least from its suggestion. Line engraving, on the other hand is essentially graphic; it consists of lines, denoting changes of plane.' More than a technique, line engraving is really a special way of seeing texture, which enables one to analyse it in three dimensions. And 'engraving is nearer to bas-relief, and therefore nearer to sculpture than to painting and drawing. The printing of the copper plate on paper is the moulding of a bas-relief. But the paper reveals a subtle aspect of the plate which escapes any scrutiny of the copper.' For these new aesthetics, see Flocon's *Traité du burin* (1952).

Joseph Hecht was a forerunner of this approach: he tried to revive relief engraving about 1949, but without success. Jean Dubuffet has also made some interesting technical experiments.

PABLO PICASSO. *The Frogs*. Illustration to Buffon's *Histoire Naturelle*. 1942.
Sugar aquatint

In England, there is a current rebirth of print making, which in the first half of the twentieth century only just survived, it being then considered a pastime, and playing a part only in illustration.

This rebirth is due to Hayter, whom we have already mentioned, and who unremittingly continues his search for new techniques, and also to Robert Erskine, who opened the Saint George's Gallery in London and in 1954 started a print maker's studio with the sole object of promoting graphic art. Among young artists, we may mention Michael Rothenstein, whose linocuts are well-known, and Ceri Richards, known for his series of lithographs, *Hammerklavier*.

Like Merlyn Evans (born in Cardiff in 1910) best known for his series *Suite verticale*, Frances Hodgkins (1871–1947) was influenced by Braque and Picasso.

Nigel Lambourne (born 1919), has produced some of the finest engravings and etchings to be seen in Britain since the war. His work has a great range including soft ground, etching and aquatint, and deep etch. He studied under Malcolm Osborne (1880–1963), whose drypoint portraits, with their monumental realization of form, have never been surpassed.

Frank Martin (born 1921) is best known for his wood engravings. Like Nigel Lambourne he has done book illustrations for the Folio Society. Another fine wood engraver was John Farleigh (1900–65), who illustrated George Bernard Shaw's *The Black Girl in Search of God*. A special place is occupied by Eric Gill (1882–1940) for his magnificent craftsmanship as an engraver on both copper and wood.

Geoffrey Clarke (born 1924), a printer, sculptor and remarkable master of stained glass, is probably one of the best known artists in England, where he has had exhibitions since 1951. His engraved work, often sugar aquatints, influenced by Klee, won him the prize for the New Figure in Tokyo in 1957.

Italian artists, whom we know from the fifth Biennale (1962) in particular, hesitate between Expressionism and Abstraction. Germany (from what was seen at the exhibition of the German Arts Council at the Folkwang Museum in Essen), has abstract artists, such as Carl Buchmeister (born 1890), and a perhaps more important artist, R. Kugler (born 1921), whose etching of a

PABLO PICASSO. *The Pipe Player*. 1956. Colour lithograph

LE LÉZARD

PABLO PICASSO. *The Lizard*. Illustration to Buffon's *Histoire Naturelle*. 1942.
Sugar aquatint

JEAN LURÇAT. *The Cock*. 1950. Lithograph

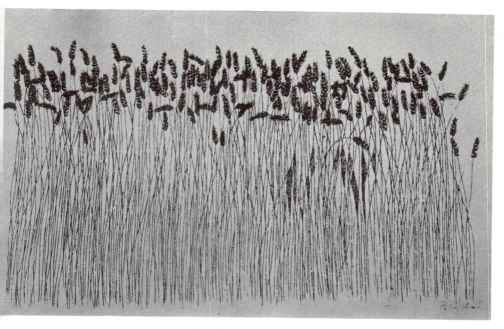

BEN SHAHN. *Wheatfield*. 1958. Silk screen print

house in ruins (1962) has a beautiful texture. We are told that the French influence is strong in Germany since 1945, and that many artists come to Paris to work under Mourlot, Visat and Lacourière. In the United States, judging from the exhibitions of the Print Council of America, presided over by Lessing J. Rosenwald, we see that beside the abstract artists there exist very remarkable figurative artists. Among these are the sculptor Leonard Baskin (born 1922), a truly significant artist; Mauricio Lasansky (born 1914), who triumphed at the Mexico exhibition in 1961, and whose head of a man with large ears is striking; Ben Shahn (1898–1969) who wanted to create his 'own realism'; and Misch Kohn, one of the greatest exponents of the technique of wood engraving.

Antoine Hoyber, a Dutchman, took part in the 1960 Venice Biennale. Having suffered in concentration camps and reflected bitterly on life and death, he has recalled the obscene graffiti of the prisoners and soldiers, and shows 'the image of man's humiliation and a call for protest' (Z. Krzisnik).

MARIO AVATI.
The Butterflies of Nagasaki.
1962. Aquatint

KIYOSHI HASEGAWA.
Tame Bird. 1963.
Mezzotint

Other Dutch artists are Eduard Flor, Lucibert, Jacobus Westerik (a surrealist), Metten Koornstra, Wouterman, Hensden (in the style of Redon), Ap. Sok, J. Biernma, O. Sting and R. Escher. We must also mention Karel Appel, a lithographer, who is said to be the author of the largest book in the world, as high as a door.

Lismonde, a Belgian artist came to print making after many years doing wall-size drawings. Philippe Roberts-Jones notes that since 1959, he 'creates surfaces which no longer have any definite limits, and asymmetry predominates in his work. His surfaces are made up of lines, often in opposition to one another, of varying thickness and concentration, which give to the masses they create their dynamism and their quality of radiance.'

On the other hand, in Austria, Kokoschka shows himself, as ever, very much against Abstraction in his recent lithographs; his *Magician* of 1952 is intended to show that the artist can get nothing out of it but a rabbit shadowed on a wall.

236

A huge country remains still practically unknown to us, the U.S.S.R. Reactions in opposite directions have occurred there; on 8 March 1963 Krushchev, in a speech which was widely discussed, declared, as Robespierre had done, that art should be '*revolutionary and militant*. Soviet literature and art are destined to commemorate . . . the great heroic days of Communism . . . The artist must see that which is positive; *art is referable to ideology*.' We have already seen some hints of the unfortunate results of this appeal for realism in art.

YOZO HAMAGUCHI. *Bowl of Fruit.* 1962. Mezzotint

However, it is undeniable that, as in Italy, in Germany, in the United States and in a variety of other countries, the art of print making in Russia is deeply influenced by the Ecole de Paris. Countless examples demonstrate this world-wide influence; but we need only mention the case of Albert Blatas who recently published in New York an album of fourteen lithographs portraying the artists of Montparnasse who had become his friends, under the title *Homage to the School of Paris*.

A FEW OTHER TECHNIQUES

As well as etching, wood engraving, the woodcut, lithography and relief engraving, mention must be made of some other techniques, some old, others only recently invented, to which artists have been attracted.

The first is mezzotint, a traditional technique which was devised by

LARS BO. *Time Passes*. 1963. Lift-ground etching

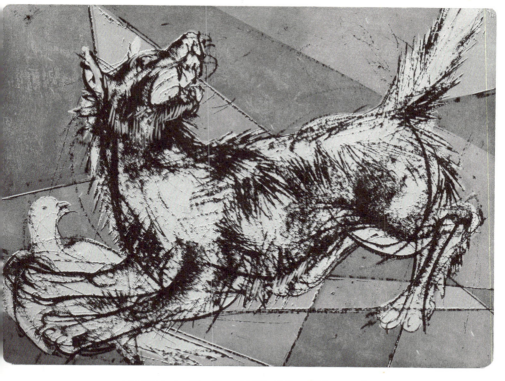

HANS ERNI. *The Dog*. 1963. Colour lithograph

Lieutenant-Colonel Ludwig von Siegen in 1642. In the seventeenth, eighteenth and nineteenth centuries, few masterpieces were produced by this technique, which in fact did not inspire very many artists. The plate is roughened with a tool known as a rocker which is passed backwards and forwards in all directions until a surface is obtained which will print a uniform black. Lights and half-tones are scraped out, thus making the picture, which is then printed. In spite of the sometimes disappointing results obtained with this difficult method, there is at present a revival of mezzotint.

D. E. Galanis (born 1882), an artist of Greek origin, who has been living for a long time in Paris and has illustrated a great many books, is one of the great masters of mezzotint, as also is Kiyoshi Hasegawa (born in Yokohama in 1891), who has been working in Paris since 1918. Both artists were working in mezzotint about 1930, with great success, thanks to their sound craftsman-

JOHN PIPER. *First Avenue Hotel, Hove.* 1939. Sugar aquatint

ship. The technique was recently adopted by Mario Avati (born 1921), who has used it to express 'a strange and devastated universe'.

As well as mezzotint, there is also the black and white or coloured linocut, which first became popular among American artists, and thanks to which Picasso started in 1958 the wonderful plates of his *Tauromachie* series.

Another artist, Fiorini, perfected a method of printing from linoleum without reinforcing the surface. This, however, gives only a limited number of fine prints. His method has since been used by a number of artists.

Silk-screen printing, a subject for which we refer the reader to Hayter's book, *About prints,* is akin both to lithography and stencil. First used in China, then in Japan, it is a very ancient process, originally used for printing on fabrics (in Lyon for example). It rose to the high rank of an original printing process in the United States, where it was rediscovered in the thirties. Today there is a Serigraph Society in New York, and there has been a silk-screen printing congress in Paris.

The method consists in drawing with greasy ink on a silk screen stretched over a wooden frame. The drawing finished, the artist applies a thin layer of size on the silk, and the size is removed from the drawn parts with a solvent. Then a sheet of paper is placed on the screen, and the artist presses the colour through the silk with a scraper. This must be repeated for each different colour.

Yet other techniques have been tried out, such as Krasno's neo-engraving with a metal-plated plastic mould, or new attempts at etching on glass in imitation of Corot.

An important phenomenon is the fever of work which recently gripped Picasso, who again took up in his line engravings his eternal themes of the artist at work and the embrace, to which he has added the theme of the picture presented to the public as if the master were seeking its approval.

POSSIBLE FUTURE DEVELOPMENTS

To conclude on a note of optimism, the successful future of the print seems well established. Prints have found a public in many different countries. In Germany they are highly esteemed and there are increasingly numerous print exhibitions.

In the United States, the sales in exhibitions organized by the Print Council have risen by two or three hundred per cent since 1959, and moreover the Ford Foundation is encouraging new experiments such as the Tamarind Workshop. In England, the public is now taking an interest in prints, and artists are pleased to feel that they are thus communicating with the public. In Chile, a first international exhibition of prints was a success; in Italy, as we have already mentioned, there is an ever growing interest in prints, for which art galleries and museums, contrary to what Pierre Courtin has written, show a very real enthusiasm. We recommend Courtin's *la Lamentation du graveur*, from which we quote, and which is an excellent text; it is witty and possibly true, providing a necessary balance to over-optimism and reminding us of the hard lot of the print maker who finds it difficult to make a living. To engrave is a damnation, he says, for it is a craft full of disappointments: 'If the tool slips, it will bury itself in one's left hand', and the artist has to spend a considerable amount of time rubbing out and scraping and polishing

241

his plate. 'The engraver does not split hairs in four, but in 256 or even 512.'

This same man has to educate the public, speak about himself at length, and explain the methods he uses, for the public knows nothing about them, the technique of engraving rarely finding a place in the school curriculum. The engraver has also to stress the difference between original engraving and photomechanical reproduction, a difference which is so little appreciated that the print market is in an unhealthy state. This is not remedied by the dealings of certain artists and publishers (the Print Council has fortunately launched the idea of an international definition of original prints). Fortunately too, the public is young and eager, and is being given intelligent help and advice by publishers who are also young, in its quest for new prints.

But what will these prints that so many await be like? Will they be abstract or realistic? Do they have to be one or the other? The wisest viewpoint is probably that of Henry Moore: 'Abstract qualities of design are essential to the value of a work, but to me of equal importance is the psychological, human element.'

BIBLIOGRAPHY

ADAM, HENRI-GEORGES. *Catalogue de l'oeuvre gravé.* La Hune, 1957

ADHÉMAR, JEAN, MLLE AUBERTY and M. PERUSSAUX. *Catalogues de l'oeuvre de Villon et de l'oeuvre de Waroquier.* Chez Prouté, Paris

AMERICAN PRINTS TO-DAY. *Two catalogues of exhibitions by the Print Council of America.* 1959 and 1962

ARGAN, G. C. and CALVARI, M. *Boccioni.* Rome, 1953

ART D'AUJOURD'HUI (L'). *La gravure contemporaine.* April 1950

BUCHHEIM, L. G. *Die Brücke.* Feldafing, 1956

BUCHHEIM, L. G. *Hechel.* Catalogue 1905–56. Feldafing, 1957

BUCKLAND-WRIGHT, JOHN. *Etching and Engraving. Techniques and the Modern Trend.* London, 1953

CAILLER, P. and LOIRÉ. *Catalogue de l'oeuvre gravé de Segonzac.* Geneva, 1958, with prefaces by Julien Cain, J. Vallery-Radot, J. Adhémar, Cl. Roger-Marx

CARLS, (CARL D.). *Ernst Barlach, das plastiche, graphische und dichterische Werk.* Berlin, 1931. 7th edition, 1958

Catalogue de l'exposition Masson. Brême, 1954

Catalogue de l'exposition Matisse. Chez Klipstein and Kornfeld, Berne, 1961

Catalogue of the Max Ernst exhibition at the Museum of Modern Art, New York, 1961

COGNIAT, RAYMOND. *Zadkine.* Paris, 1958

CRAVEN, T. *A Treasury of American Prints.* New York, 1939

CROQUEZ, A. *L'oeuvre gravé de James Ensor.* Geneva—Brussels, 1947

DORMOY, M. *A. Vollard.* 1946

GARVEY, ELEONOR M. *The artists and the book, 1860-1960.* Exhibition of the Boston Museum of Fine Arts. Preface by P. Hofer. 1961

GEISER, B. *Picasso peintre graveur.* Paris, 1955

GODEFROY, L. and LOYER, J. *Catalogue de l'oeuvre gravé de Laboureur.* Paris, 1929 and 1961. 2 vols

GUÉRIN, M. *L'oeuvre gravé de Gauguin.* Paris, 1927

GROHMANN, W. *Le Bauhaus.* Dans l'Oeil. Paris, 1957

GROHMANN, W. *Kirchner.* Stuttgart, 1958

GROHMANN, W. *Kandinsky.* Cologne and Paris, 1958

GROHMANN, W. *H. Moore.* Berlin, 1960

HAAS, IRVIN. *A Treasury of Great Prints.* New York, 1956

HAESAERTS, P. *Ensor.* Brussels, 1957

HAYTER, STANLEY WILLIAM. *A new way of gravure*. New York, 1949

HAYTER, STANLEY WILLIAM. *About Prints*. Oxford, New York and Toronto, 1962

HOEN, ARVE. E. *Munch, graphic art and painting*. Oslo, 1956–8. 3 vols

HOFFMAN, E. *Kokoschka, life and work*. London, 1946 (with catalogue 1908–45)

HOFFMAN, W. *Georges Braque, das graphische Werk*. Stuttgart, 1961

KENNEDY, E. G. *The etched work of Whistler*. New York, 1910

KLIPSTEIN, A. *Käthe Kollwitz, vez. der graphischen Werkes*. Berne, 1955

KLIPSTEIN and KORNFELD. *Hans Arp, Graphik, 1912-1959*. Berne, 1959

LANGAARD, J. H. *Catalogue de l'exposition de l'oeuvre gravé de Munch*. Oslo, 1958

LEIRIS, M. *The prints of Joan Miró*. New York, 1947

LIEBERMAN, W. S. *Matisse, 50 years of his graphic art*. London, 1957

MEYER, F. *Marc Chagall, das graphische Werk*. Stuttgart, 1957

MOORE, HENRY. (ed. with introduction by P. JAMES). *Henry Moore on Sculpture*. London, 1966

MOURLOT, F. *Picasso lithographe*. Monte-Carlo, Sauret, 1949–56. 3 vols

NAEF, HANS. *Hans Fischer*. In Graphis, no. 25, 1949

PENNELL, J. and E. *Lithography and Lithographers*. London, 1915

PESINA, J. *Moderni ceska grafika*. Prague, 1940

POMMERANZ-LIEDTKE, GERHARD. *Der graphische Zylers von Max Klinger bis zur Gegenwart All. 1880-1955*. Deutsche Akademie der Kunste, 1957

REESE, A. *American Prints of the twentieth century*. New York, 1949

ROGER-MARX, CLAUDE. *Graphic Art of the nineteenth century*. Thames and Hudson

RUHMER, E. *L. Feininger*. Munich, 1961

SCHAPIRO, R. *Schmidt-Rottluff's graphisches Werk bis 1923*. Berlin, 1924

SCHIEFLER, G. *Das graphische Werk E. Nolde*. Berlin, 1917 and 1910–27

SCHIEFLER, G. *E. Nolde, Jahre der Kampft*. Berlin, 1934

SERVOLINI, L. *Dizionario illustrato degli incisioni italiani moderni e contemporanei*. Milan, 1955

SOBY, J. T. *The prints of Klee*. New York, 1945

STUBBE, WOLF. *Die Graphik des zwanzigsten Jahrbunderts*. Berlin, Editions Rembrandt, 1962

SVABINSKEHO, Z. *Socialni Grafika*. Prague, 1902

TRENTIN, G. *Note sulla 2° Biennale dell'Incisione italiana contemporanea*. Venice, 1957

VRIESEN, G. *August Macke*. Stuttgart, 1957

WALKER, R. A. *The best of Beardsley*. London, 1948

WATSON, E. W. and KENT, R. *Relief Prints*. New York, 1945

WILLACH, SIGURD. *Munch, etchings*. Preface by L. A. Langaard. Oslo, 1950

ZAMPIETTI, P. and TRENTIN, G. *Mostra dell'incisione italiana contemporanea*, catalogue. Venice, 1955

ZIGROSSER, CARL. *A book of fine prints*. New York, 1948. Several editions

ZIGROSSER, CARL. *The expressionists*. London, 1957

ZILLER, G. *Frans Masereel*. Dresden, 1949

LIST OF ILLUSTRATIONS

The page numbers printed in bold type indicate reproductions in colour

246

247

INDEX OF NAMES MENTIONED IN THE TEXT

PRINTED IN FRANCE BY IMPRIMERIES DE BOBIGNY